Fighting for Success

About the Author

Lynne Miller has a PhD in Psychology with a postgraduate qualification in digital marketing. She began her career as a research scientist working for a multinational FMCG company. She subsequently established her own independent research consultancy, Miller Associates, successfully working with both public and private sector clients over a period of twenty-five years. In 2009, she left the New Forest in Hampshire, UK, with her daughter, Rhian, for a one-year sabbatical in Phuket, Thailand. They have remained in Thailand ever since. In 2011 she opened the internationally renowned Sumalee Boxing Gym with her daughter. Concurrently they have developed their understanding of Thai culture and Thai language. Rhian is now a qualified Thai language interpretor (DPSI Law). Lynne's son, Sam, was also involved in the Sumalee business at the outset and now lives and works in Hong Kong.

For more information:

www.sumaleeboxinggym.com
www.sumaleephuket.com

- facebook.com/SumaleeBoxingGym
- instagram.com/sumaleephuket/
- twitter.com/SumaleeBoxing
- linkedin.com/in/lynne-miller

Fighting for Success

Lynne Miller

SUMALEE

First published in the United Kingdom by
Sumalee Books

Copyright © 2022 Lynne Miller

Lynne Miller has asserted her rights under the Copyright, Designs and Patents Act 1988 to be identified as the authors of this work.

Cover Art Design by Semnitz
Typeset by RefineCatch Limited, www.refinecatch.com
Printed and bound in Great Britain by Clays Ltd, Elcograf S.p.A.

Paperback ISBN: 978-1-7398166-0-5

All rights reserved. No part of this publication may be reproduced, stored in a retrieval system, or transmitted in any form or by any means, electronic, mechanical. photocopying, recording or otherwise, without the prior permission of the copyright owners.

www.sumaleeboxinggym.com

In memory of my parents, Sheila and Gerrard Higgins
Dedicated to my children, Sam and Rhian

Contents

About the Author		ii
Prologue		ix
1	How It All Began	1
2	My Muay Thai Journey	7
3	Building a Business in Thailand: The Basics	19
4	Thai Business Partners	39
5	Building a Muay Thai Gym Team	59
6	The Signing of Saenchai	77
7	Sponsoring Muay Thai Fighters	87
8	Muay Thai Fighter Contracts	106
9	Muay Thai Promotions	117
10	Muay Thai Fighter Glorifcation and Other Anecdotes	138
11	A Change in Direction	160
12	The Unexpected Joys of Owning a Muay Thai Gym in Thailand	173
13	The Worldwide Covid-19 Pandemic and the Future	184
Epilogue		193
Acknowledgements		196
Index		197

Prologue

In the years since we opened Sumalee Boxing Gym in Phuket, Thailand, family, friends and guests have encouraged me to write about my involvement in the Muay Thai (MT) business in Thailand. As a consequence of the worldwide Covid-19 pandemic in 2020 and 2021, I have found the downtime to tell my story. This book gives a glimpse of that venture into the world of MT, the national sport of Thailand.

My story started as a one-year adventure with my daughter, Rhian, when she was 17 years of age. Twelve years later, I am still here in Thailand, having swapped my life in the UK for the challenges not only of setting up a business in this Southeast Asian nation, but doing so in the very much male-dominated world of MT.

This book describes that journey, including our experiences of working within the MT fraternity, the challenges we have faced and the reasons our business has evolved in the way it has.

The Thai business world is presented through the eyes of someone used to doing business in a more developed economy and in a professional context. For someone with my background, perhaps the greatest challenge has been making sense of it all to develop a business model that I felt comfortable with and that was viable financially.

Many businesses within the MT community struggle for a number of reasons, lack of investment in the sport being one of the main ones. The modus operandi of most traditional MT gyms does not follow a traditional business model. These gyms have evolved based on a system of patronage. They have been slow to adapt to the opportunities presented by the growth in international interest in the sport. In consequence, their vulnerability has never been more evident than during the time of the worldwide Covid-19 pandemic.

The pandemic has left the sport in Thailand ravaged and it will take many years to recover, if it ever does. The experiences of building our business described in this book will explain why MT businesses have been particularly hard hit. A significant proportion of MT businesses are dependent on sending fighters to promotions as their primary source of income. They have never diversified by developing other income streams. By the time the ripple effect of the pandemic is over, at least two years of not being able develop fighters will in itself present a challenge many MT businesses will find difficult to overcome. A number of notable MT businesses have already failed and at the time of writing this book, the pandemic in Thailand is not over yet. As ever in any crisis, there will be winners and it will be interesting to observe how the pandemic will shape the MT business of the future.

Not everyone will agree with the conclusions and observations I have made in this book. Nevertheless, they are mine seen from my perspective as a MT gym owner. Setting up the Sumalee business has been one of the greatest challenges of my life and one of the most satisfying. We have faced many obstacles and we have come up with our own individual solutions to these. Starting as a traditional MT gym, we have evolved and are well placed within the broader wellness sector. Whilst retaining MT at the core of the business, we have broadened our offerings to include a yoga programme and a nutritional support package. It has been all consuming and, at times, emotionally draining. Without the expertise and support of Rhian beside me throughout the journey, survival would have been much more difficult.

Although only directly involved in the business for short periods, my son, Sam, has been a pillar of strength too. He is now working as Head of Nutrition for a large fitness group in Hong Kong. He played a key role, alongside Rhian, in setting up Sumalee's nutritional programme.

Would I do it all again? Undoubtedly, yes! If starting again was necessary, it would be comforting to do so with the knowledge and experience I have now gained. As a friend of mine once said, 'At least you are out there living life.' This, we have certainly done. Despite the difficulties, the process has led to an amazing adventure most do not have the good fortune to experience. Financially and given the Covid-19 pandemic, I will probably end up being worse off than when I started. As a person though, I am definitely richer.

Thai culture can be often difficult to comprehend. We have seen the best of it and we have seen the worst too. There have been many experiences that would have been better not to have had. On the other hand, we have been the recipients of warmth and generosity beyond our wildest imagination. Over the twelve years of building the Sumalee business, we have created a community of people from across the world who have trained at our gym. A number of our students have described this experience as life changing. There can be little more gratifying than to know that something you have created, alongside your team, has enhanced someone else's life.

Behind any successful business is a strong team. In the beginning at Sumalee, staff turnover was high. By putting the right systems and support in place, we have a long-standing and stable team who have been with us for many years. They are the backbone of our business. Their lives have been turned upside down by the pandemic and we have done our best to keep going and support them during this time. It is hoped that we all will be rewarded for our endurance and patience with a return to normality, albeit a different normality going forward, even if the recovery is a gradual one.

Chapter 1
How It All Began

People who visit our Muay Thai (MT) gym in Phuket, Thailand, are extremely curious about what led to the decision to open Sumalee Boxing Gym. Perhaps they hope to find inspiration in our backstory. They dream of doing what I have done. There is a long history behind it – it certainly didn't happen overnight.

If you are under retirement age, and unless you are very fortunate, finding a financially viable way to carve out a living on a tropical island in Asia is a goal only a few are able to achieve. Phuket is not everyone's dream of paradise, and it is not perfect in every way, but for most it's about as good as it gets.

I first came to Thailand in 1983 when I visited Bangkok and Pattaya, both of which were very different places then compared with now. It was in Pattaya that I had my first experience of watching MT, more commonly known as Thai boxing.

Pattaya was a small fishing village until the 1960s, when it became a rest and recuperation destination for American soldiers during the Vietnam War. Meeting the needs of soldiers looking for distractions from their onerous wartime duties dictated the direction in which Pattaya was to develop. It became known as a place where men in particular would have their every desire accommodated.

Although Pattaya was already renowned during the 1980s, it was nowhere near as developed as it now. In 1983, although perhaps difficult to imagine now, it still had a villagey feel to it. The bars were local style and many had boxing rings in the centre. Fighting provided entertainment for the customers, the aim being to keep them in the bar for as long as possible. The modern-day equivalent are bar girls, whose job it is to keep the customers entertained whilst encouraging them to purchase more alcohol.

As with the majority of people who visit Thailand, I was entranced by what I found here. The easy-going charm of people belies much of what hides below the surface. Life here appeared carefree and for many years I longed to return.

I didn't have the opportunity to visit Thailand again until 2000, although I did travel elsewhere in the Asia region whilst working as a research scientist for a major international corporation. During the intervening period, I was focused on building my career and family. I started my own company in the UK in 1985. I had my son, Sam, in 1988 and daughter, Rhian, in 1992.

I found the Asian countries I visited culturally intoxicating and have read extensively about them my whole life. In terms of the interest sparked within me though, Thailand was on another level. To live and work here was a dream I imagined would be impossible to fulfil.

Investing in a Time-Share Changed the Course of My Life

The story of the genesis of our business in Thailand would not be complete without mentioning the role played by an investment in the Marriott Vacation Club. The decision to invest took place long before any notion of staying in Thailand on a long-term basis was formed. It was, however, a crucial turning point that ultimately took my life in a new direction.

To travel long haul as a family in the late eighties or early nineties was not as common as it has become in the new millennium (pre-Covid-19 of course). It took my partner and me some years of travel closer to home in Europe and the States before we felt confident enough to travel far with young children. When Sam and Rhian were 9 and 6, respectively, we felt we were ready. Initially we did trips to Singapore, Kuala Lumpur and Penang. These excursions were primarily made possible by our decision in invest in the Marriott Vacation Club in December 2000.

As my partner and I both had our own businesses, it was convenient for us to travel at Christmas, when traditionally little work is done in the UK for at least ten days. We transported ourselves annually from the depths of a British winter to the warmth and sunshine of Asia. On our first trip, when we stepped off the plane in Singapore, my son couldn't believe how beautiful it was with bougainvillea in full bloom all around. His first words on exiting the airport were 'Wow, this is just like paradise.'

Like me, both children became quickly hooked on Asia too. On our first trip as a family to Thailand in December 2000, we stayed at the Marriott Royal Garden Riverside Hotel. This was a beautiful resort at the edge of Bangkok sitting on the banks of the Chao Phraya River.

Anyone who has ever travelled in Asia will know that the standard of hotels and service is above and beyond any expectation derived from travelling in Europe and even the United States. For a family of four, these hotels are expensive especially during peak season. With this in mind and having paid USD300 a night for the four of us to stay in one room during our forthcoming stay at the Laguna Beach Resort in Phuket, when we saw that Marriott were extending their Vacation Club brand to a new resort in Phuket, my partner was especially interested in going to the presentation.

At that time, time-shares had a poor reputation mainly because of stories out of the Balearics and the Canary Islands about hard-selling time-share touts. However, we felt that Marriott was a brand we could trust and, in any case, they offered a free meal at their Japanese restaurant that for a family of four on a budget was a once-in-a-lifetime offer!

We went along to the presentation at the appointed time. We were impressed by the standard we could expect for our family vacations should we invest. Having already been cooped up for several nights in the same room as our kids, we found the two-bedroom, spacious villas, with all amenities necessary to make a family holiday cost effective and run smoothly, extremely appealing. The villas were to be located at the JW Marriott Resort & Spa in Phuket, which was only partially built at that time. Nevertheless, they showed a mock-up of the resort and presented us with the details of the scheme, which made the concept even more attractive. We quickly did the math and it seemed like a no-brainer: participation in the scheme offered the promise of having a standard of vacation that would otherwise be difficult to afford.

I am a *carpe diem* sort of person. If I weren't, I would not be in the favourable position I am in now, living an enviable lifestyle in Thailand. Of course, there were risks but in reality, we felt the risk of Marriott not fulfilling their promises and obligations was low. It's all about calculated risk and we were not disappointed. We immediately bought one week at the Phuket Beach Club at £12,000. Within the next year we bought another week at the same price.

We completed the purchase and our stay in Bangkok, having availed ourselves of the enjoyable free incentive meal at

Marriott's Japanese restaurant, and went on to Phuket for our planned stay at the Laguna Beach Resort. Whilst in Phuket, we took the opportunity of visiting the JW Marriott Resort & Spa, even though at that time only the main reception and the Cucina restaurant were built and open.

When we arrived, we could hardly wipe the smiles of satisfaction from our faces regarding our purchase because, as anyone who has ever visited the resort will know, the lobby/reception area is stunningly alluring.

The Marriott Vacation Club has an annual maintenance fee, which in 2020 was approximately THB35,000 per week of ownership. This gives seven nights in a well-equipped and spacious two-bedroom villa, which sleeps up to six people. The resort sits beachfront in the more undeveloped northern end of Phuket. It is aesthetically stunning, well maintained and equipped, with acres of tropical gardens and an unbeaten standard of service. Of course, we didn't know just how attractive the resort would be when we invested, as it wasn't completed, but our instincts proved us right.

We had our first family holiday at the Phuket Beach Club in December/January 2000. By happenstance, the only year we had missed coming to Phuket in December was in 2004, the year of the tsunami. That year we had made a reservation to visit Phuket but at the last minute changed our plans, choosing a cruise instead.

Through various incentives given to us by Marriott and Interval International, we were often able to come to Phuket twice a year. As time went on, we became more involved in life here and made many Thai friends. Rhian started to learn Thai and it was for her to become more proficient in the language that we decided to stay in Thailand for one year in 2009.

It was during one of the many vacations at the Marriott that we met the MT fighter Deachkalon Sor Sumalee. This in turn led to our passive enjoyment of the sport into a more active involvement in the MT community/business in Thailand. If it had not been for that spontaneous decision to buy into the Marriott Vacation Club scheme in December 2000, our journey to establishing Sumalee as one of the most successful MT gyms in Thailand would never have started.

The decision to invest in Marriott not only changed my life but it changed the future trajectory of my son's and daughter's lives too. My daughter now runs Sumalee with me and my son is based in Hong Kong working as a nutritionist. This was an opportunity that came about as a result of working with us at Sumalee for two nine-month stints after completing his first degree.

Like many hotels around the world, the JW Marriott Resort & Spa in Phuket is now suffering unprecedented difficulties resulting from the closure of Thailand's international borders because of the worldwide Covid-19 pandemic. It is my heartfelt wish that they are able to overcome these difficulties as they have played such a large and important part in my own life and those of my children.

Chapter 2

My Muay Thai Journey

During our regular trips to Phuket we often visited the old boxing stadium at the top corner of Bangla Road to watch Muay Thai. In truth, I understood little of what was going on but as a spectator sport, it is tremendously exciting and one can't help but admire the bravery of the fighters. I was keen to know more, especially about the backgrounds of the fighters.

The Bangla Road stadium was wonderfully intimate with an electric atmosphere. It closed around 2007. I am not sure of the reasons but one of them may well have been that it was not big enough to accommodate the burgeoning number of tourists and the growth of interest in the sport.

The old stadium was much more representative of grass-roots MT than its newer counterpart, Bangla Boxing Stadium on Sor Kor Road in Patong, which opened around 2009. (In the interim period a temporary stadium was set up as, until the Covid-19 pandemic, the show never stopped!) Fortunately for the investors, the opening of the new Bangla Boxing Stadium coincided with an explosion of interest in MT tourism in Phuket and Thailand as a whole.

It was during a visit to the temporary stadium that we met and struck up a friendship with the fighter Deachkalon Sor Sumalee (nickname Oron). Incidentally, all Thai people have a nickname as well as having a given name and a family surname. MT fighters have a third name, usually conferred by their gym, which is their fighting name.

Oron spoke only a few words of English and we had few words of Thai. However, he did manage to invite us to see him fight. This was in August 2008. He came into the ring wearing the Bangla championship belt but unfortunately, he lost the fight. This was in the days when I thought that particular belt meant something and I felt terribly sorry for him when he lost. Now I know this particular belt is just for show and I understand why he was so unconcerned! The championship belt is paraded at the Bangla Boxing Stadium at least once in every programme and is for entertainment purposes only, designed to generate audience excitement.

We returned to the UK the next day with no expectation that the chance meeting would lead to anything further. Oron had different ideas, however, and kept in contact by email and telephone. The exchanges were very short because of the language barrier but he continued to ring frequently.

At that time I knew nothing about a MT fighter's career path. I now realise that Oron's fight career in Thailand had passed its prime and he was searching for new means of making a living. He had a young son and had been fighting in the Chiang Rai area where MT was not valued and fight purses were small. He was struggling to survive.

Soon after our visit to Phuket in 2008, I decided to take a one-year sabbatical. The years 2008/2009 heralded the start of yet another worldwide financial crisis, which particularly affected government spending and allocation of money to local authorities in the UK. Although we worked for many notable international corporate clients, most of our contracts came from within the public sector nationwide and there was a strong indication that the amount of money they had available for expenditure on research would be cut back. Rhian, who was 17 at the time, was also at a crossroads. Since her first visit to Thailand, when she was 8 years old, she had shown an aptitude for the Thai language, increasing her vocabulary on every visit. She was tremendously keen to take this further. It therefore seemed like an ideal opportunity for both of us.

Over the years, my travels to developing countries made me very aware of how fortunate I was to have been born in a country where education was free. At the time I studied, university was also free and I had benefitted from six years of this. This free education provided me with a passport to achieve career success. Many of the Thai people we met during our vacations in Thailand expressed a desire to travel overseas but did not have the means to do so. I had already formulated a plan that at some point I would help a Thai person visit the UK. When Oron, with the help of a Thai friend who spoke better English than he did, sent an email early in 2009 asking me if I would help him become a trainer in the UK, I decided he would be the person I would help.

Oron came from a poor community in the countryside of Ubon Ratchathani, in the Esaan region of northeast Thailand. Like many fighters (Thai and foreigner), Oron's upbringing was unsettled. When his father was no longer able to care for him, he took Oron to what was to become a highly successful and well-rated gym, Sor Sumalee Gym (SSG). Over the years this gym produced many champions including Panomrunglek, Lamnamoon, Superlek, Jompoplek and Deachkalon (Oron). Although Oron was not quite as well known internationally as these fighters, he nevertheless had achieved considerable renown within Thailand itself.

Oron was the ideal candidate for the opportunity to come to the UK. He would not have been able to achieve this under his own steam but was nevertheless likely to gain considerable benefit from the experience. And he did. My decision was divorced of any plans to open a gym, which had not even occurred to me at that time. I had never even seen a MT training camp at that stage and didn't fully understand what it was.

With the help of Sean Toomey (gym owner, promoter and World Boxing Council (WBC) representative in the UK), I was able to secure a place for Oron to pass on his knowledge at Sean's Lumpini Gym in Southampton, near to my home in the New Forest. If it had not been for Sean's help, Oron's trip to the UK would not have been possible. Prior to setting this arrangement up, I sought Oron's reassurance that he was not tied into any contract with a gym in Thailand. He was able to give me that.

As I had already planned to stay at least a year with Rhian in Thailand from August 2009, it was agreed with Oron that he would come to the UK in the summer of 2010 when I returned. This gave me the chance to get to know Oron during the year before facilitating his trip.

During our year in Thailand it had been our intention to do volunteer work. Research undertaken beforehand only threw up volunteer tourism, which I had considerable ethical reservations about. Consequently, when we arrived in Thailand, Oron became my volunteer project!

At the time Oron was living and working in the old Bangla Stadium. This had been converted into a makeshift gym. All his possessions were in a cardboard box and his bed was a red plastic vinyl sofa in the gym area. In all honesty, it was a bit of a shock to find out how he was living and I must admit to having some reservations to begin with. Over the year, however, as I got to know him better, I found he was able to focus on his training if he needed to. When he had a fight coming up, which he did usually at least once a month, he trained consistently beforehand for at least two weeks.

Although confined to fighting only at the Bangla Stadium in Patong during this period, his fight record that year was good.

During our stay, I prepared Oron for his trip to the UK in a number of ways. I introduced him to social media and assisted him in creating a Facebook account. I had business cards made for him and encouraged him to give these to any foreigners he trained in Thailand. I made a rudimentary website for him and I filmed all his fights. In common with many MT fighters of his generation, surprisingly little video footage survives of the days when he was at his peak. The aim was to try to increase his international profile, which was more or less non-existent at the time. (Although social media sites have since burgeoned in Thailand, in 2009 uptake was low and few Thais had smartphones.)

It was through our support of Oron that we became more acquainted with the MT world. We frequently went to the run-down gym where he was based to watch him train students.

We had based ourselves in the Nai Harn area, in the south of Phuket. Apart from Nai Harn Gym, there was little around at the time other than MT boxing gyms. Having watched Oron train his students, I felt that most of the exercises involved were within my capability. I was fairly physically fit for a woman of my age and was keen to continue my fitness regime. With the encouragement of some MT trainers we randomly met when out one evening, Rhian and I decided we would join one of the local MT gyms. I particularly enjoyed group classes as I found exercising with others provided me with the motivation I needed.

We trained at that gym almost every day during our initial stay in Thailand. It was a tremendously liberating and enjoyable experience. By the end of the year I felt fit, slim and confident. In fact, I felt so positive about my experiences at the gym that when I was offered the opportunity to invest in it, I honestly couldn't believe my luck and was more than keen to sign up.

I had given the gym owner various pieces of business advice over the course of the time I trained there. He was a fighter and had been brought up in a traditional Thai gym, with no commercial business experience. I was naive enough to believe that he wanted me on board to provide some business acumen. It turned out his sights were set well short of that.

Oron in the UK

My sabbatical in Thailand was cut short in May 2010 when I was called back to the UK to work on a research project. I took Oron with me as promised. I covered all his expenses, which included the flights and his living costs whilst in the UK. It would have been impossible for him to cover these expenses on the small income he received from fighting and helping out at Bangla Boxing Stadium. Fight purses in Thailand are generally low.

Oron was an entertaining fighter, which was why he attracted our attention in the first place. Not only was he immensely skilled as a fighter but, known as the King of Esaan Dancing, he incorporated a traditional Esaan dance into his pre-fight routine.

His ability to entertain the crowd placed him hugely in demand. Even so, his maximum fight purse at Bangla Boxing Stadium at that time was around THB8,000, which was equivalent to £160 then. This formed most of his monthly income and with this, he also had to provide for his wife and child in Chiang Rai. On an income of this size it would have been impossible for him to self-fund any part of a trip to an expensive country like the UK.

Prior to leaving, we had to go the British Embassy in Bangkok to obtain a visa for Oron, which required him to have a face-to-face interview. This was an exciting journey in itself. It was at the time of the mass political mobilisation, from March to May 2010, when Thailand endured the most violent confrontations since the protests against military rule in 1992. Over this period at least ninety people died and more than 2,000 were wounded in clashes between security forces and antigovernment protesters led by the United Front for Democracy Against Dictatorship (UDD), also known as Red Shirts.

Arson attacks in Bangkok and elsewhere caused billions of dollars of damage. Large areas of the capital were barricaded, including the area where the British Embassy is located. Taxis were not able to pass the barricades so we had to make our way there on foot. I remember being shocked at the threatening nature of the barricades, built from hundreds of tyres, barbed wire and fearsome-looking bamboo spears, and at the fierceness of the people manning them. It was nerve-racking walking through there.

The interview at the embassy was followed by a wait of several weeks before we knew whether Oron had been approved for the visa. When the news came through and Oron could see the sports visa stamp in his passport, he could hardly contain his excitement.

Oron was transfixed by the whole experience of travelling to the UK. He had travelled by air before but only on a few occasions. He certainly had never been on a jumbo jet, and Dubai International Airport, where we stopped over, was a different world to him. By contrast, Heathrow Airport was less of a surprise for him, looking more like a third-world airport than anything found in Asia.

Oron was fascinated with what he found in the UK. What

made the biggest impressions on him were: the clean and litter-free countryside; the long days (arriving in the British summer, he was incredulous that it was still light well into the evening); and the automatic dishwasher we had in our home!

As a psychologist with an interest in how people react and behave, I was equally fascinated with observing his reactions. It gave me a great deal of pleasure to have been the facilitator of his trip. For me personally, if this were all that had come out of the trip, it would have been enough to make it all worthwhile.

It's interesting to see your own country through the eyes of someone whose country is different in so many ways. It helped me appreciate many things I took for granted, especially our planning laws, lack of encroachment on our countryside, enforcement of bylaws such as littering, and the respect for others our social consciousness gives us.

It made me feel vastly proud of my country and especially proud of the New Forest and the City of Southampton with its magnificent cruise terminal. As it happened, however, the trip was to give so much more than this on many levels.

During our six-week stay in the UK, Oron assisted by passing on his knowledge at Sean's gym every day. His work ethic was impeccable. During his time there, he also gave a one-day seminar that was attended to capacity with twenty-six students.

Oron was also invited to give a seminar at Benfleet Muay Thai in Essex. He'd met and trained a student, Colin Gosling, in Phuket whose home gym was Benfleet. When Colin heard Oron was going to be in the UK, he arranged with the owner of Benfleet Muay Thai, Bradley Goldberg, for Oron to hold a seminar there.

The reception and welcome we received in Benfleet was second to none. Benfleet Muay Thai is a small, well-run family-oriented gym. It has produced a number of well-known fighters in the UK scene including Reece Thompson, Evan Foster Jays and Joshua Ridgwell.

When we visited, all three were quite young and their parents were very much involved in their careers. They could not have been more hospitable and kind to both Oron and myself. So much so, that when we left Benfleet after a farewell meal on the Sunday, Oron cried for most of the journey home. He was extremely touched by the welcome they had given him.

Something that made a huge impression on him was that as we were leaving, all the team came out of the restaurant to wave him goodbye. As a result of this there was a slight hold-up to the passing traffic. Oron was incredulous that the other drivers had waited patiently until we pulled away.

Sean worked hard also to find Oron a fight whilst he was in the UK. At short notice, because someone had dropped out, Sean found him a fight at 59kg, which was several kg below Oron's usual fighting weight at that time. The fight was a six-man tournament, hosted by Simon Audley, and took place in the Adelphi Hotel in Liverpool in July 2010. The fight purse was a winner-takes-all at £2,000. This was twelve times more than the purse Oron usually fought for in Phuket at that time and approximately as much as he earned in a year.

Oron dedicated himself to the preparation for this fight, running every day and adapting his diet to attain the weight loss required. On our drive up to Liverpool from Southampton, Oron was so weak he spent the whole journey lying in the back of the car counting the miles off one by one. I have to say that if I had known at the time how dangerous such rapid weight cuts are, I would have been a lot more worried about his condition than I had been.

When we arrived the day before for the weigh-in at the Adelphi Hotel, most of the other contestants had no idea who he was or what his credentials were. Fighters such as Oron, whose careers were at their peak prior to widespread social media use, are often not known at all outside Thailand.

One contestant, Rung Karnphan, a Thai who had been living and running a MT gym in Scotland for many years, was very well aware of who Oron was. Rung was one of the favourites to win the tournament. He told us later: 'When Deachkalon came in, none of the others knew who he was but I knew. I also knew that he was more than likely going to be the winner of the tournament.'

It was an exceptional show, incredibly well organised and attended. Each leg of the tournament was three rounds. A Scot named Douglas McAdam was the master of ceremonies, a popular choice whose commanding presence and ability added to the excitement of the occasion. Liam Harrison was one of the show's commentators.

Oron fought Jonno Chipchase in the quarter-finals and won. In the semi-finals he fought Rung Karnphan and won. In the final round Oron fought Keith McLachlan. This was a close and exciting fight, so much so that after three rounds the judges declared a draw and requested the fighters to fight another round. Keith was so tired he was unable to come out of the corner. Oron was declared tournament champion, winning the £2,000 fight purse and the championship belt.

In actuality, Oron was far more gratified with the belt than he was with the money. In his Thai career, although he had done well and been runner-up on a few occasions, he had never won a Thai stadium belt. He slept with that belt beside him for many nights afterwards.

It was a rewarding experience for both Oron and me. Sam later made a highlight video of Oron's fights during this tournament, which can be found on YouTube. Watching it, to this day, still makes the hairs on the back of my neck stand on end. There's no question about it, in his prime Oron was a skilled tactician in the ring.

Considering I had had no prior involvement or experience in MT to have brought a fighter over and to see him achieve so much, I more than compensated for any of the costs involved. If someone asked me to list my lifetime achievements, this would come very near to the top of the list.

Oron's success at the 59kg six-man tournament ricocheted him into high visibility within the UK MT scene. The fight was live-streamed and there was a lot of interest in it as the best UK fighters at that weight were included.

Oron spent days afterwards monitoring his 'rating', as he referred to it, on Facebook. He received many friend requests from fighters in the UK subsequently. It is worth bearing in mind that this was before the days of Yokkao-sponsored shows, so relatively few Thais had ever come over to the UK to fight.

His trip also coincided with the burgeoning growth in social media, so news about him travelled well. Oron was fortunate enough to have two other trips to the UK during the time he was involved with Sumalee, to fight on shows in Scotland organised by John O'Brien.

Oron retained all the earnings from his trip to the UK, including his fight purse and the tips Sean Toomey gave him. On his return to Thailand, he bought his first brand-new motorbike. It was a very rewarding experience for me and I was more than pleased to have helped him establish a name internationally and to obtain this new vehicle. For me, the trip to the UK with Oron was the last time I was able to dwell on the pleasure that MT in itself can bring. It was a time unfettered by business concerns, ethical/moral considerations and cultural/interpersonal differences. All these matters quickly came to the fore when we returned to Thailand.

On our return to Thailand, I joined in partnership with the MT gym in Nai Harn, Phuket. It was always the plan that I would return to Thailand and work to help develop this business. I had persuaded the co-owner of this gym that given Oron's new prominence within the UK MT scene, it would be a wise decision to employ him as a MT trainer in the knowledge that he would attract UK students who wanted to train with him. Oron therefore joined with my new business venture.

In any event, I left the business within six months over significant concerns about the way it was run and my position. When I left, Oron was given a choice; he could continue to work at the gym if he had no further association with me. If he couldn't accept that, he was required leave. It was Oron's decision to leave. Perhaps if Oron had been able to stay in that business on terms that were acceptable to him, Sumalee may never have come to be.

Once Oron's hand was forced so that he resigned, it was somewhat inevitable that Oron, my daughter and myself would go our own way. To open our own gym had not been my original intention but since we were all here with no other purpose, it was the logical next step.

As mentioned previously, Oron's formative years of training as a MT fighter were at the Sor Sumalee Gym (SSG) in Ubon Ratchathani. It was with the permission of the owners of SSG that we chose to include 'Sumalee' when we named our gym Sumalee Boxing Gym. When we opened in 2011, their gym had long been closed.

Khun Sumalee was the wife of the owner. She is fondly remembered by the fighters who trained there, for being very stern but kind too. Apparently, she would often visit the gym during training sessions, bringing fruit for the fighters. Sumalee is a relatively common name for Thai women and many people local to our gym refer to me as Khun Sumalee.

Chapter 3

Building a Business in Thailand: The Basics

Having taken the leap to come to Phuket, my goal was to improve and breathe new energy into my lifestyle. When I was offered the opportunity to invest in a financially struggling MT business, I took it. I genuinely believed I could make a positive contribution to the business whilst simultaneously ticking some items off my bucket list.

Although I learnt a lot during the course of the experience, I soon realised that investing in an existing business was a considerable mistake for me. I left after only six months of joining the partnership and together with Rhian, we built up our own MT business.

At the time of writing, Sumalee Boxing Gym (now known as Sumalee Phuket) has been in operation for nearly ten years. Whilst MT remains at the core of the business, Sumalee has evolved into a wellness business, providing a place where the physical, mental and nutritional needs of our guests can be met.

It is only in writing this book that I have realised, in my enthusiasm to find a way of furnishing a better work/life balance, how incredibly naive I was at the outset. It is unlikely that I would have taken so many risks if I had been starting a business in the UK, even though it would be much easier for me to source trustworthy advice there. There are many barriers to foreigners sourcing such advice here, with language being the most significant.

I have been fortunate because in the long term my gains (both financial and on a personal level) have outweighed my losses. Despite the economic hardships created by the Covid-19 pandemic, which is ongoing at the time of writing, this would still be my conclusion. If anything, the opportunities and challenges created by the impact of the pandemic have enhanced rather than diminished my overall experience here.

As well as providing practical advice and guidelines, this chapter is a 'warts and all' exposure to many of the mistakes we made along the way in the early stages of building our business. It is my hope that in writing about them, others aiming to follow a similar path will be prevented from making the same mistakes.

Our early vision was that Sumalee would be a traditional MT gym business. Much of our experience of building the Sumalee business can, however, be applied to any small and medium enterprises (SME) in Thailand. Where this is not the case, it will be clear.

It's easy to be seduced by the apparent *saabai, saabai* (very relaxed) attitude that prevails in Thailand. Visitors yearn to be a part of that, not realising that what lies below the surface is often complex and difficult to comprehend.

Many people who visit Thailand want to stay for as long as possible. The fortunate few are able to do this without needing to generate income here. For many others, this is not possible. To stay, they have to make a living. There's little employment available for foreigners here. Foreigners are prohibited from many occupations, which must remain the sole domain of Thai people. Businesses are reluctant to employ foreigners because of the extra costs involved. To avoid these, where possible, businesses prefer to draw their workforce from the Thai national population. This is why many who have had no previous experience of building a business take their first steps in Thailand. Some succeed and succeed well. Failure rates, however, are high.

The costs involved and the requirements of setting up a business in Thailand are seductively low compared to doing so in a more developed economy. For example, to set up a MT facility in the UK would involve either the purchase or lease of space, which can be prohibitively expensive, especially if it is in an urban setting. Meeting health and safety, licensing, insurance, building and fire regulations would also be expensive and challenging.

This is not the case in Thailand. It is important not to let this fool you into thinking that running such a facility (or any other business) in Thailand is easy. If you want to make a success of it, it is far from easy. There are many other challenges to be met and the competition for 'tourist spend', whether foreign or domestic, is harsh.

There is a saying often used by foreigners in Thailand: 'If you want to leave the country with a million dollars, arrive with 20 million dollars.' Sadly, many entrepreneurs lose all they invest. A good rule of thumb is not to invest any more than you can afford to lose especially in a country where you have little control over extraneous factors that might impinge on the business.

Views regarding what makes a successful business are varied. In the MT gym business arena, some who love the sport feel that developing renowned stadium fighters should take precedence over profit. This is laudable but fails to make allowances for the hidden costs of living and working in a foreign country (eg. visa, work permit, health insurance, costs of education where children are involved etc.). It also fails to take into account the business operating costs and responsibilities to provide all staff with security, all too often overlooked here.

If the business is not profitable and ergo not viable, time here will be limited and you will be seriously out of pocket when you leave. Indeed, those businesses that ignored the basic principle of viability were amongst the first to disappear during the Covid-19 pandemic.

Although not impossible, few entrepreneurs in Thailand go on to create substantial businesses. Nevertheless, if you are smart and able to negotiate the many stumbling blocks along the way, you can make a reasonable living and have a good lifestyle in Thailand. This is reward enough for most entrepreneurs and can outweigh the disadvantage of reduced earnings potential compared to home.

In my opinion, the first pre-requisite of starting any enterprise in Thailand is a basic grounding in the Thai language. If this is not attainable, you should at least have someone whom you can trust, without reservation, to act as a reliable interpreter. This person should be well known to you. They should also have no vested interest in the outcome of any proceedings.

Finding such a person is difficult because of the commission system that operates in Thailand. This is where a person who makes an introduction or smooths negotiations receives commission if a financial transaction takes place. This is rarely a transparent process so it's wise to be well aware of it. With hindsight, I now realise that people who appeared to be helpful to me in the early days were benefitting financially. This is not necessarily wrong, but it should be transparent.

It is important to research Thai culture and understand its impacts on business. Thailand has a very high proportion of SMEs and, of these, the vast majority are family owned. Nepotism is the main recruitment methodology. Recruiting the right person with the right qualifications for the job is of secondary importance and severely limits the growth potential of many businesses here.

In developed countries, respect in the business world is usually based on qualifications, positions held, accomplishments etc. In countries where the business environment is predominantly populated by SMEs, perceived 'power' (usually wealth) commands the most respect. I have never been asked about the suitability of my qualifications or past career in any business context I have been involved in since moving to Thailand.

It's also important to know at the outset how long you intend to stay in Thailand. Many invest heavily in businesses here only to find that when their circumstances change (for example, having a family), staying in Thailand is no longer a viable proposition. Be clear about what your long-term plans are and scale your level of investment accordingly. Businesses do sell here but unless it is profitable, selling is a challenge. Not unexpectedly, during the Covid-19 pandemic this has been an even greater challenge for foreigners seeking to off-load flailing businesses.

The first thing you will need to do is identify what type of business/sector to invest in.

This is much more difficult than it appears, especially if you want a good chance of being successful. There are many 'copy cat' businesses in Thailand and competition levels are high. Not only do many investors in Thailand have no previous experience in business (it is alarming how often this is the case), they invest in areas of business they know nothing about. (The latter point applied to me but at least I did have the experience of running a successful business elsewhere.)

All too often when people invest in a business in Thailand, decisions are emotional rather than cognitive.

On a tourist island such as Phuket, most foreigner-owned businesses target the tourism sector. Prior to the worldwide pandemic, this sector offered the best chance of success because the domestic market has different preferences and most have little disposable income. However, the pandemic has fundamentally changed the business landscape, perhaps forever.

In the business-to-business (B2B) sector, it's wise not to be misled into thinking that the absence of a particular service means there is a gap in the market. All too often it means that the service is not valued and consequently there is no demand for it.

Traditionally many Thai businesses in tourist areas such as Phuket were successful by virtue of their location alone. Their marketing strategies were internally focused and mainly involved ensuring that new tourist arrivals were channelled in their direction by paying handsome commissions to gateway service providers such as taxi drivers. Market research via the internet has meant that many traditional Thai tourism businesses (e.g. factory shops, tour booths etc.) are floundering as these days business is driven by information accessed long before the tourist arrives.

To a large extent, choice of business to invest in will depend on interests and budget available. It will also depend on what the competition is doing. In heavily saturated sectors, such as restaurants, guesthouses and coffee shops, a unique proposition will be the key to success. A market appraisal or Strength, Weakness, Opportunities & Threats (SWOT) analysis is an important but often missed first step.

The tourism sector in Thailand is heavily oversubscribed and, of course, seasonal. Seasonality is something investors repeatedly fail to take into consideration. A visit during high season when everything is full to capacity is misleading as the revenue stream is not constant throughout the rest of the year. This must be taken into account when preparing a business plan.

Before investing in any business, it is important to fully understand it. Inexperienced entrepreneurs often overestimate income and underestimate outgoings. Do the math. Calculate what your income needs to be to meet your liabilities and understand if the business you intend to invest in can deliver. The tourism sector is subject to external factors that are beyond the business's control. A safety net needs to be built in to take account of this. During the twelve years I have been in Phuket, many MT gyms have come and gone because the owner didn't fully understand the financial dynamics of the business.

One of the biggest mistakes investors here make is that they do not have enough money to invest initially and they either underestimate or are ignorant of the ongoing costs involved. Consequently, their business is sub-standard, making it non-competitive and unsustainable. Seasonality of income flow and time necessary to build a successful business are additional constraints. Many new businesses here are doomed to failure before they even open their doors to customers.

If a foreign investor needs financing, the options for obtaining it are limited. Foreign banks are reluctant to lend money for business start-ups in Thailand. Thai banks are reluctant to lend to foreigners and, like all banks worldwide, will lend only against assets.

This means that an investor in a start-up business in Thailand needs to be able to self-fund (or fund via other investors) and have sufficient resources to support them whilst the business becomes established and during undulations in income stream. Covid-19 has raised an even uglier spectre. The Thai government has limited resources to support their own nationals, let alone foreigners.

The bottom line is that if a business in Thailand is to be viable in the long term, it needs to have substantial financial reserves. This is true wherever you are in the world but particularly so in a country where there is nowhere to turn if things go wrong.

The business proposition needs to be set apart from others in the sector. Being one of the crowd is not a good market position. It should be a proposition that can adapt and evolve to stay ahead of the game. The market here is competitive and new businesses are opening all the time.

The initial concept for Sumalee was a traditional MT gym. Since we opened in 2011 there has been an explosion of interest in MT, fuelled by social media and smartphone ownership. The growth in demand has led to a multitude of gyms opening in Phuket. Not recognising the need to evolve would most likely have led to business failure.

Having completed all the research, and come up with a unique and viable business proposition, the next stage is to turn the dream into a reality. The three main avenues to do this are:

1. Buying an existing business outright
2. Investing in an established business
3. Starting afresh

My own experience has been with the last two options.

Whichever way is chosen, it's important for entrepreneurs/investors to proceed with due diligence. Legal advice should be taken from a lawyer who is independent of the matters in hand. Lawyers should be vetted, with personal recommendation being one of the best ways of ensuring a trustworthy lawyer is found. Doing things in the right way may cost more in the short term but in the long term, potentially save a lot of money and heartache. In your enthusiasm to get started, don't overlook the need to think carefully about any contract. Thai nationals/lawyers in Phuket will have had a lot more experience of drawing up a contract than you have.

If the contract involves a lease on a fixed term, think very carefully about what that means. For example, if the term of the lease is not long enough, you can find yourself building up a business only for it to be taken over by the landlord before you've derived enough benefit from it. I have witnessed this happen on many occasions. If the lease contract is not legally binding, it's easy to find yourself in the situation where the owner seizes the land/property back before the term of the lease is over. This often happens too and if terms are not sewn up properly at the outset, there's nothing you can do about it.

If I hadn't had a legal contract when I invested in my first business, I may have found myself in difficulty. Even having taken the precaution of drawing up a legal contract, I did cut corners and was too trusting of others. Fortunately, my mistakes did not cost me too much financially. I have seen others lose everything they invested either because they believed they were infallible or they were too trusting of the person they were dealing with. It is well to always remember that the business landscape in Thailand is vastly different to the one we may be used to. Additionally, it's not our country so the odds are against us.

Social media is helping to provide naive investors some protection. I believe it helped me exit the first business I invested in relatively unscathed. If it had been five years earlier, when social media channels were in their infancy, my story may have been very different too. Nevertheless, it is advisable to remember that in Thailand, social media can only give limited protection because of the strict defamation laws here.

A final piece of advice here is that if you yourself work in the business, make sure you have a work permit. It's surprising the number of foreigners who work in Thailand but do not have one. Although few actually get caught, the consequences if you do are severe and may well involve a few nights in a local prison. After this, if your case is not resolved, you will be deported from the country and not be allowed to return for a considerable number of years, if at all. It is advisable not to be persuaded to work for someone else either unless they provide a work permit. Digital nomads, of which the numbers are increasing, and volunteers are also required to have a permit to work in Thailand. Having a work permit increases the cost of working/running a business here and you will be required to pay personal taxes. In the long run, however, abiding by this law can save you an unpleasant experience and a lot of money. It could also save you from losing your business altogether.

A work permit can only be obtained through a Limited Company (Ltd Co.). This is normal practice in many countries where foreign employees must be sponsored by a company. Thailand is no different in this respect. A foreigner who wants to work has the option of finding a company to sponsor them or they must set up their own company. A foreigner cannot work legally as a sole proprietor or in a business partnership. It is only through a Ltd Co. that the criteria to obtain a work permit are met. To work legally in Thailand, one option for a foreigner is to invest in an already established business where at least 51% of the shareholders are Thai nationals. The other is to open a Ltd Co. with a suitable Thai business partner and allocate at least 51% of the shares to them. Often, the Thai business partner is not an investor or only a minor investor in the new business. (There are some exceptions to this if you are an American citizen.)

People often ask me if I have ever been subject to extortion since running a business in Thailand. This has never happened to me. If you/the business follow the local laws, there are no grounds on which you can be extorted.

Buying an Existing Business

I do not have any personal experience of this first option but I do have some advice. The main difficulty centres around estimating the true value of the business you are proposing to buy. The culture here is for the business owner to give a figure based on what they would like to get for the business rather than its true value. This happens in the housing market as well. Where small businesses are concerned, vendors rarely obtain an independent evaluation of the business.

Although things are rapidly changing in Thailand and businesses are required to be more accountable, estimating the value of a business based on turnover and profitability is more often than not very difficult. A significant proportion of small businesses here do not declare all their income for tax purposes. Accurate records of income versus expenditure are frequently not even kept. Money going into the business account (if there is one) will not be a true reflection of the business turnover. In these circumstances, it is easy for the turnover figures to be manipulated to the best advantage of the vendor. Annual accounts submitted to the revenue department are only a partial indication of the financial health of the business.

In situations where the business being sold has land or building assets, then market valuation of these assets is certainly possible. It's the value-add of the business itself that is not easily quantifiable. The issues involved in the purchase of a business with significant land and buildings assets are beyond my remit, as I do not have experience with purchasing such a business.

If you are purchasing a business that occupies leased land or buildings, be sure to check over the terms of the lease and ensure the agreement is registered with the Land Office. If the lease is not registered, you have no legal rights if the landlord wishes to evict you, even without good cause. I have seen this happen many times. When a business becomes established and profitable it is not unheard of for the landlord to reclaim their rights over the land or the property before the end of the agreed lease.

Although I didn't buy a business, I did buy a company when we embarked on the Sumalee project. It was a company that was no longer trading but the groundwork in setting it up had been done. This meant we could begin trading without delay. Something I didn't do, but should have done, was to check that the company had no liabilities. All company papers, financial documents, end-of-year accounts etc. are written in Thai. The foreigner is reliant on the people advising them to point out if there are any discrepancies as most small-business investors would not go to the expense of getting the papers translated. As the company was purchased from our lawyer, I didn't feel the necessity to do so. Although in our case the damage was small, there was some unpaid value-added tax (VAT) that had to be cleared.

Investing in an Established Business

Most, but not all, of the comments in this section relate to my experience of investing in a business owned by a Thai national.

I have first-hand experience with this and it's an area where I would advise extreme caution. Even the solicitor who drew up the contract for me advised me not to go forward with the investment. I didn't take the advice and regretted not listening to her.

There are so many factors to consider when taking this course and I hope to draw your attention to as many as possible. The main thing to be aware of is that most SMEs in Thailand are run as family businesses.

There are also some special considerations that are particular to investing in a MT business. The owners of most MT gyms are likely to have different education, business and life experiences compared to a foreign investor. In tourist areas such as Phuket, boxing professionals own many of the MT gyms. During their formative years they were brought up in gyms where life was often regimented and tough but also where they found a close-knit community. Traditional Thai gyms have a unique business model and are not dependent on paying customers to survive. The proceeds from gambling usually form a significant part of the income stream. This brings with it inherent problems not least of which is its unpredictability. Many MT gym owners have limited experience with customer-facing business models. In consequence, their business philosophy is different. This causes many problems. I have witnessed many MT business partnerships break down because of it, including my own.

In the business model the MT fighter is most likely used to, the gym owner is an autocrat. They have complete and unquestioned authority over how the gym is run. Giving up this role is hard for a gym owner who has been used to running his own show.

On the surface, it may appear that inequality between men and women in Thailand is based on economic circumstance. However, this is not the case at all. Gender inequality runs deep within the fabric of Thai society. This is particularly pervasive within the MT community, which is predominantly a male domain. Women investing in an established MT gym have this to contend with as well as everything else. (In my own case, the fact that I was a woman was outweighed to some extent by my age. I was older than anyone else in the business and age is very much respected in Thai culture. My age gave me considerable advantage.)

In deciding whether investing in an established business is a suitable option for you, you need to fully understand:

- ✓ The business background and history of the person you plan to go into partnership with. All too often visitors to Thailand enter into business partnerships without really knowing enough about the others involved in the business. I did this myself. Any history of a failed partnership with a previous foreign investor should raise a red flag. (I ignored this warning sign myself to my peril.)
- ✓ What the motives are for the owner selling a portion of the business. (Business owners rarely sell part of their business unless they need funds for one reason or another.)
- ✓ What the business looks like from the inside. (Behind the scenes of the business I invested in, I saw discordant factions operating, which made the day-to-day running of it challenging.)
- ✓ How the business is managed.

- ✓ What the ethics and values of the business are. (The business/culture in Thailand is very different from more developed economies and this can cause conflict.)
- ✓ What the relationship is between the existing owner and the staff. (In the business I invested, all the staff were 'his people'. If things go wrong, as they did, you can find yourself isolated.)
- ✓ How decisions are made. (If you are partnering in a MT gym business, the existing owner will most likely be used to running things without deference to anyone else.)
- ✓ What your role within the business will be and this needs to be clearly laid out in any contractual agreement. (Many business owners are looking for investors only and will hope to exclude them from decision making in the long run. This can only work if you are confident that the existing partner will manage your investment well.)
- ✓ Whether there is a development plan for the business and how this will be funded.
- ✓ Whether you and your prospective business partner have the same aspirations and values for the business.
- ✓ Whether you and your prospective business partner 'speak the same language'. By this, I don't just mean native tongue. In the business I invested in, the partner and I brought different skills to the table. His expertise and knowledge, and they were significant, was in MT. Mine was the experience gained from running a successful and profitable business for many years beforehand and the 'softer' business skills of marketing/customer service/relations/business admin. Whilst I respected his knowledge,

he didn't respect mine because he didn't understand the importance of these skills. This was a huge area of discord between us.

Should you be like me and ignore the advice not to invest in an already established Thai business, these would be my recommendations to you:

- ✓ Spend several months being involved in and observing the business at close range before proceeding with an investment.
- ✓ Conduct a thorough audit of the financial health of the business and make sure you are fully aware of any liabilities the business has relative to its assets.
- ✓ Get an independent valuation of all land and property assets.
- ✓ Only invest in a limited company, which will ensure you are not personally liable for any debts accrued by the business.
- ✓ If the business is not already a Ltd Co., get it changed as part of the handover process.
- ✓ Employ a lawyer to draw up a legally binding contact for you. This is especially important. It will involve a cost but could potentially save you a considerable amount of money in the long run.
- ✓ Once the business is a Ltd Co., unless you can speak and read Thai fluently (the preferred option), make sure there is someone within the business (or your own lawyer) whom you trust and who is able to act in your interests. They should have access to all company documents/information during the whole course of your involvement with the business. This is important.

✓ Have this trusted person with you when you sign any papers relating to the company that are written in Thai.

Starting Afresh

In this scenario, you have your well-researched concept and have come up with a unique business proposition. There will now be many decisions and steps involved. I can only provide guidance on the route we took, which required us to set up a Ltd Co. and to obtain premises from which to operate the business.

As mentioned previously we set up a Ltd Co., which we bought from our lawyer who offered to sell us an established company. A caution with respect to this course of action has already been noted.

The recommendations regarding the distribution of the shareholding are, like everything else in Thailand, constantly changing. The one thing that never changes is that at least 51% of a Ltd Co. has to be owned by a Thai national/s. (The rules are different for American citizens but I am unsure of the details.)

If done properly, with the input of a good lawyer, this is perhaps not as risky as it may seem. Shareholders need not be directors of a company and consequently need no part in the day-to-day operation of the company. This means they have no access to any aspect of the financial running of the company.

In all honesty, I am not an up-to-date expert in company law and current practice relating to this. It is better to take advice from a trusted lawyer. I would, however, recommend that you choose a Thai national who is not related to either yourself or anyone in the business, unless it is in a professional capacity. If you can find someone who is independent of the business, this is the best course to take.

Setting up a Ltd Co. is a legal process and is subject to Thai law. To release a shareholder, the process is far simpler if they resign. It is possible to ask the Thai national to sign the release papers so you have them if you need them. Unlike when I signed them unknowingly, it is ethical to make this process transparent.

To create Sumalee, we needed a substantial piece of land. Purchasing was one option but unfortunately land in Phuket at the time was becoming increasingly expensive. Prices for land have continued to rise as Phuket has become more developed. At the time of writing, prices have held despite the Covid-19 pandemic. The long-term viability of tourist businesses, however, is in question. Consequently, with hindsight, perhaps leasing the land was in the long term the better option for us anyway. In leasing the land, we took the precautions advised earlier on in this chapter and ensured the lease was registered with the Land Office. We have been extremely fortunate with our landowner who has never interfered with us or our business and has been very accommodating of our needs. Others are not so fortunate.

If your business project involves employing a construction company, as ours did, either select an established, reputable company or obtain references about the company you intend to use. If the building project is substantial, my recommendation would be to set up a written contract drafted by a lawyer. Make sure all plans are drawn up by a professional architect. Overall, the construction of our site went well but I have known many other investors to have problems, including losing substantial sums of money to a contractor who disappeared or being left with building problems that are difficult to rectify. We did have some relatively minor problems with contractors ourselves, but this was nothing in comparison with other stories I am aware of. In our case, we used a contractor to build fitted furniture in the rooms we hire out. The contractor completed the first six rooms to a high standard without any problem. When we paid him THB180,000 in advance for the next batch of rooms, we didn't see him again. We went to his place of work, which we found abandoned. Using our lawyer, we issued a writ threatening him with court action if he didn't either complete the work or return the money. He ignored the writ. There was little more we could do, short of taking him to court, which would have involved considerable expense for us.

To give you an idea of the scale of the construction project, the land we leased contained one structure only at the outset.

We now offer a Muay Thai, yoga and nutritional programme. At the time of writing, our facilities include a MT gym, yoga shala, sixteen rooms (with different grades to suit various budgets), massage shala, swimming pool, equipment shop, office/reception area, international restaurant and vegan café.

Some readers may feel that this exposé on business start-up in Thailand is too cautionary and that it suggests dark undertones to doing business in the country. This is not my intention. My intention is to make people aware that things work differently here.

Whether your interest in Thailand is as an investor or even as a tourist, I urge you to pay attention to the core values of any business you closely associate yourself with. It is a constant source of amazement to me that the values people hold so dearly at home are completely forgotten about when they are in Thailand. Of course, it's hard to look behind the veneer of any business, and even more so in Thailand where language barriers make it difficult to obtain any information about a business, either written or verbal. But take a good look at what's going on. Don't go in blindly. How is the business run? How are the staff treated? What rights do they have? Are they protected under Thai employment law? In the case of MT gyms, what kind of contracts are their fighters on? Is the business making a contribution to their own country by paying all the relevant taxes or is the owner looking after himself and his family only?

Thailand is still a relatively poor country, with a gross domestic product per capita twelve times lower than Switzerland and more than eight times lower than the United States in 2020. In order for this situation to improve, businesses must take the lead ethically. Ask yourself if the business you are buying from/investing in has either the capacity or the willingness to do this. The answer should guide you in your actions. The choices you make should be no different to the choices you make at home.

As a business investor, if you get it right, you can have an enormously satisfying and profitable business whilst at the same time make a contribution (even if only a small one) to the development and growth of the country. If you cut corners and are prepared to turn a blind eye to what's going on around you, you end up losing your moral compass and you risk losing everything you've invested.

Chapter 4
Thai Business Partners

(Author's note: The names of the business partners involved have been changed to protect their identity and privacy. The events described are based solely on my perspective of what took place. The purpose of providing the information is to inform other investors of issues they may encounter with business partnerships in Thailand.)

The gym business I invested in initially was not already set up as a Ltd Co. and my investment in it was dependent on changing the company to Limited status. I insisted on this to reduce any personal financial liability should the company run into problems.

My business partner (hereafter referred to as Dtae) was compliant as far as this was concerned. Dtae had an ongoing arrangement with a local lawyer, who advised him free of charge, as he owed Dtae money. This may appear to be an unusual arrangement to people living elsewhere.

In Thailand obtaining a formal loan can be difficult so informal loans/borrowing is not out of the ordinary. Where such arrangements exist, the debt of favour often far exceeds the value of the amount originally borrowed.

All matters relating to changing the status of the business were handled by the existing accountancy service and lawyers used by Dtae. I trusted them to do this and didn't envisage any reason not to do so. Of course, all the necessary documents were written in Thai and, in hindsight, rather stupidly I signed them without understanding what I was signing.

This was a mistake and went against the basic business principle of never signing a document not read or understood. I remember at the time naively saying, 'It's a good job I trust you guys.' In fact, what I had done, without knowing it, was sign away my shares in the business. Such practice is often used in Thailand where the principal investor is only a minor shareholder (e.g., when a foreigner is the principal investor in a company but cannot own more than 49% of the shares according to Thai laws). It protects the principal financial investor by enabling them to remove shareholders in the event of a problem. It is a practice, however, which should not be used against a shareholder who is also a major investor. Whatever the circumstances, any shareholders required to sign a share transfer document should be made aware of what they are signing and the reasons for doing so.

In the event, the fact that I had signed the share transfer document was of little significance as I left the business of my own accord. Should this not have been the case, I could potentially have lost everything.

When it came to preparing a contract relating to my investment in the business, fortunately for me I employed more common sense and used a lawyer of my own choosing. The lawyer was Thai, had been educated overseas and spoke fluent English. She laid out the terms of my investment in the business very clearly in both English and Thai following a meeting of Dtae, myself and our respective lawyers.

After the meeting, my lawyer asked to speak with me privately. She advised me to think extremely carefully about investing in the business, stressing that gambling was hugely prevalent within the MT community and that debt was commonplace. Needless to say, I thought I knew better, and I ignored her advice. At that time, to the best of my knowledge, Dtae was not a heavy gambler.

If Dtae had debts at that time, I was not aware of it, apart from a relatively small bank loan taken out in his name, which he told me about. The company itself was set up from scratch and had no outstanding liabilities. I had open access to all bank accounts and felt confident that nothing underhand was taking place. Throughout my short tenure in the business, I felt my business partner was open and honest regarding financial decisions and income. I never found anything to lead to any suspicions in this regard. The difficulties we had lay in other areas of operating.

Thailand is a structured society with a paternalistic monarchy. The King, who is the constitutional head, is at the top of the hierarchy. There is a saying in Thailand, that all others are like dust under the King's feet. Everyone must prostrate themselves to the King, even the prime minister. Everyone in Thailand knows their place. The *wai*, an endearing and attractive gesture consisting of a slight bow with hands pressed together in a prayer-like fashion, is a mechanism by which order is expressed in everyday life. There are many rules to the *wai* and careful observance of how a *wai* is delivered tells you the exact hierarchical relationship between those involved in the exchange.

Every aspect of Thai society is a microcosm of the wider hierarchical system. The hierarchy/social structuring exists in education, national government, local government, business and society generally. How this hierarchy is played out in a Thai person's life has a major impact on how they conduct themselves. Imagine coping, without preparation or training, with the huge transition in status that comes with moving from a low position in the hierarchy (young fighter in a Thai gym) to a much more elevated position (gym owner). Dtae had been able to achieve this through the help of another foreigner.

Traditional gyms were institutionalised in the way they adopted this hierarchical structure. Dtae, because he had no experience with any other way of managing, brought this with him to his own gym. He had absolute authority within the gym. No one ever challenged or questioned him. If they did, their tenure in the gym was usually short-lived.

He had had sole control of the gym for five years prior to my investment/involvement. I understand that his previous investor had allowed him to make the major decisions regarding the business. It was understandably difficult, therefore, for him to accept any challenge or questioning by me of the decisions he made.

His knowledge of MT and the fight side of the business was, without question, superior to mine. Given his background and lack of business experience, he had undoubtedly come a long way and the business was beginning to become established by the time I joined. However, it wasn't profitable and there was much work to be done for the business to grow and develop. When I joined there were no systems or processes in place to manage the customer-facing side of the business. There was no office, no computer, no booking system, no accounts package, no social media strategy, no method for collecting payments online nor even a rigorous procedure for answering emails.

Since opening, Dtae used foreign staff to assist but didn't have even the basics in place, such as a work permit or contract of employment, to assist or motivate them. Most were inexperienced in business themselves and obtaining free

MT training was their prime reason for being there. They were underpaid, under-motivated and not properly supervised. There was a lot of work to be done to get the back-office systems to even a minimal operational level.

At first Dtae was open to the suggestions I offered for improvement. He was keen to make the business more profitable and proposed that during the first year of our partnership neither of us take a salary. In my enthusiasm for the business to reach its full potential, I accepted his proposal. I was still running my UK-based research company, so I earned enough money to support me from there. I assumed he supported himself either from money accumulated from the business in earlier years or from the money I had invested in the business. I didn't question it.

I raise the issue about salaries because I want it to be known that I received no payment or financial benefit for all the effort, expertise and financial investment I made into that business. It is without dispute that I left the business in a much stronger position than it was when I went into it. When I arrived in September 2010 to take up my position as partner in the business, there was one customer staying there. When I left in May 2011, turnover had increased exponentially and overflow accommodation was being used to supplement the on-site accommodation provision. The purchase of Saenchai (see Chapter 6), which would not have been possible without my investment, and the gym's improved online systems and presence inarguably played a large part in this.

Despite Dtae's initial receptiveness to my ideas for growing the business, he quickly became resistant to change. Perhaps I was trying to move too quickly, or it was due to our very different ideas on the direction we should go in. Tensions soon started to emerge. When I reminded him that I had spent many years as a business consultant, his response was, 'Don't boast.'

The way money was spent was a huge area of tension. I felt confident that all money coming in and going out of the business was accounted for. I nevertheless felt resentful that when it came to making financial decisions, my business partner had complete autonomy whereas I had none. I always had to ask his permission, no matter how small the expenditure was. He had absolute control over all expenditure and disbursements. If he wanted to reward a trainer or fighter for good performance, he could make that decision and use gym funds to do it. If I wanted to do the same, it had to come out of my own pocket.

There were many instances where Dtae would agree to something only if I paid for it out of my own pocket, rather than the business's. All foreigners working in Thailand must have a work permit. If they are caught working without a permit, they will be deported immediately and the business will be fined. Everyone in the business was well aware of this. In real terms and relative to how much the business was turning over, the cost of the work permit is not high. The business needs to have, per working foreigner, at least four Thai staff registered under the social security system. The business had eight registered at the time, so there would be no extra cost involved in this respect. The cost of the permit itself was THB6,000 (at the time £120 pounds). A business visa was also needed. The cost to change my non-immigrant O Visa to a business visa would have been around THB25,000 (£500 pounds), depending on which agent was used to undertake the dealings with the immigration department.

When I discussed the matter, I was told, 'You can have a work permit, but you have to pay for it yourself. . . . It's not coming out of the business.' This gave a clear signal of the extent to which my contribution was valued over and above my financial investment in the business.

Another example was my suggestion to include yoga on our schedule of classes. At that time, many gyms were diversifying in one way or another to grow their market share. Phromthep Muay Thai (now closed after a prolonged disagreement between the foreign and Thai business partners) was offering nutrition-based support to their customers. Tiger Muay Thai, Phuket Top Team and AKA Thailand all started mixed martial arts (MMA) programmes. To start to diversify the business and set us apart, I suggested adding yoga to the programme. Dtae was resistant to this. His vision for the business was as a MT fight gym only. He had no aspiration other than for the business to become known and well respected as a fight gym. Given his background, this was an understandable and worthy aspiration, although very difficult to achieve. The gym did not have a long history of producing well-known fighters and faced considerable competition from better-established Bangkok gyms. Nevertheless, my business partner was prepared for yoga to go on the programme, but only if I paid for it out of my own pocket. Initially I planned to do this but realised that any further investment of my time and energy into that business would be wasted in the long run.

Incidentally, those MT gyms that failed to diversify fared worse than others during the Covid-19 period. MT, being a contact sport, was one of the first and most prolonged business shutdowns the government imposed during the first lockdown in March 2020. One of the main outbreaks of Covid-19 in the country was traced back to Lumpinee Boxing Stadium in Bangkok and the repercussions for the MT community were harsh. Already perceived by some Thais as a sport that was not for them, this did nothing to improve its image. In consequence when MT gyms could re-open albeit dependent on the local market, there was no rush to take up the sport. Those MT gyms without other income streams were left standing at the baseline.

At the time I invested in 2009, the customer base at the gym was around 90% male and 10% female. There was a strong desire to increase the proportion of women training at the gym. The motive behind this was to attract more male customers to the gym! Attractive women training at the gym were flagrantly used in social media campaigns as magnets to draw people in. Coming from a background where this approach to marketing was frowned upon, I found it difficult to tolerate.

Another area where there were tensions was with respect to customer service. Shortfalls in this regard are encountered Thailand-wide and certainly were not unique to that business. There were stark contradictions. For example, there was a policy within the business at that time to keep the cost of apparel reasonable so that everyone could afford to buy T-shirts and shorts. Given that the clothing featured the gym's logo, this approach made good business sense. In fairness too, there were many examples of Dtae's great generosity to customers, such as giving away free merchandise, especially if they were influencers such as gym owners in other countries. But there were also incidents of mean spiritedness that were embarrassing to be associated with.

There is a consumer protection service in Thailand but it appears to operate at a much more strategic level – dealing with labelling, advertising and contracts, rather than with consumer complaints on the ground. Things we take for granted coming from more customer-focused societies, such as a returns policy in retail outlets, do not exist in

Thailand generally. As a rule of thumb, once you have handed over money in Thailand, you will not get it back. There are exceptions to this of course but most businesses in Thailand operate in this way. It was certainly the policy operated in the business I invested in. I remember a young customer who was not well off wanting to return a pair of shin guards, still in their wrapping and clearly unused. He was not allowed a refund. The belief was that the customer wanted to return them because he had seen them cheaper at an equipment store elsewhere. I felt very uncomfortable in those situations and, as the native English speaker, I was used as the messenger.

It became clear within three months of joining the business that my role was seen solely as an investor. Any contribution further than this was no longer welcome. Financial contribution is something that can be easily conceptualised. Years of education and experience are something that is more abstract and is difficult to appreciate if you don't respect the value of it. It would have been possible to remain in the business adopting a back seat without any involvement in the day-to-day running of the gym. It was difficult for me to do this without compromising my own integrity.

The mechanisms for dealing with conflict/differences of opinion in Thai culture are very different to those used in the West. A Thai person's instinct is to avoid it and ours is to try to tackle it head on. Communication had begun to break down, so I asked Dtae to meet with me to discuss how we could move forward. His response was: 'You are not the police, you are not my boss, you cannot tell me what to do.'

With such a response, I knew there was no way forward. To be frank, it was like being in business with an adolescent. I know, I have had two of my own! Communicating with an adult who is behaving like an adolescent is perplexing. I have experienced this many times here and I believe it stems from an education cut short. The latter stages of an education involve studying subjects, such as advanced mathematics, sociology and philosophy, that are crucial to the development of abstract thinking. Abstract thinking allows a person to deal with concepts not immediately present and also helps a person learn how to empathise.

With no shared vision for either the day-to-day operation of the gym or its future direction, our ability to work together was irrevocably compromised.

A provision of the contract drawn upon investing in the business was that, should I decide within one year that the business was not suitable for me, all my initial investment would be returned to me less a THB500,000 goodwill payment. According to these terms, I informed Dtae of my desire to withdraw from the business. I requested a meeting to discuss the financial arrangements. It was a short and awkward meeting with no pleasantries. Dtae informed me how he intended to reimburse me. He made arrangements to repay my investment over a four-month period and he adhered to this arrangement.

I made every effort to leave the business on good terms. I had learnt very early on in my career that, in business, it is not wise to burn bridges. I even sent a message to him offering ongoing help with his business, as I knew I would miss being part of it. I didn't receive a reply.

After I left Dtae's gym, a couple of other gym owners approached me. I offered to work with one of them as a marketing consultant for a year. After which I would decide if I wished to make a financial investment depending on how well we worked together. He told me it wasn't my marketing skills he was interested in. A young fighter from Liberia had approached him offering to do the marketing in exchange for free training! At least he was open and honest in telling me that he was only interested in a financial injection into the business. Needless to add, the discussions between us did not proceed further.

Prior to investing in the business, I had the best time training and meeting people there. I made my investment with a genuine desire to help Dtae grow the business. At the end, he showed no compassion or empathy for my situation. We have never spoken again since the day I met with him to discuss the arrangements for my exit from the business. On my part, the reason for this was that I could not come to terms with the heartless and dismissive way in which he had behaved. I had uprooted my life and brought a large amount of money into Thailand to invest in his business. My contribution led to a huge positive outcome on the business's fortunes.

In the short period I was involved in the business, we had accrued THB800,000 profit. This was split evenly between us. When all the math was done and taking into account my THB500,000 goodwill payment, I came out of the business with a loss of THB100,000. This was a small amount compared to that which some people lose when they invest in a business in Thailand. It is not unusual for them lose all they had invested. Nevertheless, I had provided business advice and assistance for over a year and had been actively involved in the business as a partner for six months. I received no remuneration at all for that. In the end, I didn't even receive a thank you or any acknowledgement whatsoever for the step up I had given to his business. This was the reason I have never felt inclined to speak to him again.

I did, however, contact him about an incident at the stadium immediately after the meeting to discuss my gradual exit from the business. Owners of MT gyms are not required to pay an entrance fee for either of the stadiums in Phuket. About a week after our meeting I went to the stadium to support a fighter I had sponsored for a long time. On arriving at the stadium, I was told by the security there that I had to pay even though technically I was still part-owner of the gym. The way that this was executed was quite threatening with the security guard puffing himself up and blocking my path. I knew that the man carried a gun, which made the situation even more uncomfortable as I am sure the reader will understand. I questioned the security guard about this, and he advised me that he had received a call asking them to prevent me entering free of charge. My consternation wasn't about the money but about the principle involved. I wrote to Dtae asking him why this had been done. He never replied.

The business was run in a vindictive manner. I knew this. During my time there, we had sponsored a fighter for a short period. The fighter received a better offer from another gym so decided to leave. The fighter subsequently had an exciting matchup arranged. The fight did not go ahead. Knowing this, I was not surprised about the decision to prevent me entering the stadium free of charge.

It was also of no surprise to me that when we opened Sumalee, an attempt was made to prejudice local promoters against us. They were asked not to provide Sumalee with any matchups. Fortunately for Sumalee, our Thai business partner and head trainer was also popular with the promoters locally and they refused to accede to the demand. There was no other option but to accept this. The only thing that could be done was to stipulate that our fighters were never to be matched against fighters from my previous gym. Over the course of the nine years that Sumalee has sent fighters to local stadiums, there have only been three matchups with the other gym. In all cases I believe this came about without their actually realising what was happening. I am more than happy to report that on all three occasions our fighters won.

It's difficult to remember what I felt when I extricated myself from the business. There was some anger initially and certainly regret, but the greatest feeling was one of disappointment. I was despondent that I couldn't make it work, as I do not cope with failure well. I was extremely disappointed in myself for making such an error as to invest in the business in the first place. Moreover though, I was disappointed in Dtae as I genuinely expected more of him. Looking back, however, perhaps I put too much pressure on him to change too quickly. Perhaps it wasn't that he didn't want to change. Perhaps everything about his background and the way his personality had been formed didn't allow him to change.

When I left Dtae's gym it was not my intention to start another MT business. Several circumstances, however, led me to decide that this would be the right move for Rhian and me. We had made a brave decision to stay in Thailand after our one-year sabbatical. Now we were left with no purpose. The position of the fighter in the gym I invested in was made untenable. Opening our own facility was the logical next step. This started my journey into another MT gym business with another business partner from the MT fraternity.

Establishing Sumalee

The relationship this time was quite different from the previous enterprise. The new business partner (hereafter referred to as Som) was not an investor in the business and had no executive role within it. Consequently, many of the causes of tension experienced in my previous business did not come into play this time. Som was a salaried employee of the company and his responsibility was to oversee the training as Head Trainer (HT) and to take care of the fighters, using his contacts within the MT community to achieve this.

In the main and with some guidance, Som took care of these responsibilities well in the early stages. During the period he oversaw this side of the business, Sumalee brought on some talented fighters who appeared in some of the best promotions around at the time. Som worked hard to promote the business and was a committed and supportive trainer. He didn't let his fighters down.

The unwritten agreement I had with Som was that if he stayed in the business for the period of the ten-year land lease we initially took on, he would be rewarded with one million baht at the term of the contract. This would have given him enough money to return to his home in Ubon Ratchathani, purchase some land and build either a home or a small gym of his own.

Som was involved in a very tempestuous relationship with his 'wife', who was ten years his junior. I use inverted commas for the term 'wife' as it is used even if the couple are not legally married. (Unfortunately, the dowry system that still exists in Thailand prevents many poorer couples from officially getting married, which in turn affects their long-term commitment to a relationship.) Som was not legally married to his partner but they did have a child (hereafter referred to as Nong), who was a one-year-old when we opened Sumalee. My family and I formed a close relationship with Nong over the years as we had known him since he was born. When he was old enough, the business paid for Nong to attend an international nursery school, followed by an international primary school.

Unfortunately, the ups and downs in Som's relationship with his wife impacted his performance in the business. In common with many MT fighters, he did not have effective strategies for coping with his emotions. Instead he would dull them with alcohol. His position as HT placed him as a role model for the other trainers and soon they followed suit.

This led to many tensions amongst the training staff. I had seen where this led at my previous gym and it was made abundantly clear to Som that such behaviour would not be tolerated at Sumalee.

Running in parallel to these issues within the gym, Som's partner was pressuring him to put weight on me to give them a greater return from the business. The gym was getting busier and she believed this was solely attributable to Som's success and reputation as a fighter/trainer. This is a common misperception amongst HTs in MT gyms. Their demands become unreasonable and have led to innumerable breakdowns in business relationships.

Both Som and his partner were unable to appreciate the soft skills and marketing that had been used to build the reputation of the gym as a training centre of excellence. They also failed to take into consideration the amount of money that had been invested to build the facility, as well as to get it up and running. They came to believe that they should be getting a larger slice of the income cake. They only saw the money coming into the business and had no idea what the outgoings were or indeed what the initial investment was. They also failed to consider that the education of their child was being paid for. At that time, the business wasn't profitable enough to support this cost so it came out of my personal funds. I also invested a lot of time, as did members of my family, in taking Nong back and forth to school; as well as the input we had out of school hours. If sustained, this early input would have given him the building blocks to better opportunities in his life.

I became of the opinion that the pressure on Som from his partner was increasing. There was a lot of evidence pointing to this, which it would be unfair of me to disclose. Many of the demands being made, such as funds for her to open a restaurant, were clearly coming from the partner.

Unpleasantness over one thing and another started to become a daily occurrence at the gym. We had been open for about four years by this time and over this period the family of Som's partner had gradually moved into the area. They, as well as their friends, became involved in the tensions. It is hard to relive what happened on a daily basis but things like threatening posts on social media, disruptive behaviour inside and outside the gym, rude messages and poor job performance stemming from alcohol abuse started to increase to an intolerable level.

I tried hard to reason with Som. I made it clear that I was not prepared to indulge this behaviour with the associated atmosphere in and around the locality of the gym. I gave him a choice. I required him and his partner to apologise for their behaviour in order to move on. If he was not prepared to do this, then sadly he would have to leave the business. I gave him a week to think about his decision.

He spent all that week in a haze of alcohol. During the time, I met with him on several occasions and urged him to think carefully about his decision. At the end of the week, however, he told me he had decided he would leave the business. I believe he and his partner misunderstood their position. They requested the company papers immediately when he told me of his intention and contacted the company lawyer believing we would need to buy them out of the business. The lawyer informed them that as they were not investors in the business, which was not yet profitable anyway, they were not eligible for anything.

I did, however, pay him a sum of money in recognition of his contribution to establishing the business. He used the money to make a down payment on a car, which he lost within eighteen months being unable to keep up with the payments.

In regard to the ongoing payment of his son's school fees, there was no doubt in my mind that I would continue to make them for the duration we had the business. He was only four years of age and had no part in his parents' behaviour. Within a few days of Som's departure from the business, the school contacted me. They told me that Som's partner had arrived to collect Nong from school (something she had rarely done beforehand) and told them he would not be returning. Som called me to say he planned to open his own gym and Nong would be brought up there. That gym has never materialised. After leaving Sumalee, Som went to work as a trainer in one of the larger gyms on the island. He stayed there until Covid-19 forced the gym to downsize and so he became temporarily unemployed. Left with no income and two children to support by then, during that period he sold street food. Ironically, at the time of writing, we are coming to the end of the ten-year lease we originally signed with our landowner. If Som had stayed with Sumalee, he would have been about to receive the payment of one million baht that was promised to him.

It was an especially difficult period in Sumalee's genesis. Knowing that Som had come from a very troubled family background, his attempt to cling onto the temporary stability his partner gave him was understandable. She made him feel happy at the time and Buddhist philosophy encourages focusing on the moment. What is not understandable is that he and his partner took away from their son the opportunity provided by a good standard of education. They did this in the belief they would get a 'quick fix' of money out of a business they had never financially or fully invested in. I feel this is unforgivable. What is also deplorable is that Som allowed people around him to use social media in a derogatory way against me personally, my family and the business. He also encouraged most of the trainer team to leave with him (see Chapter 5) and tried to put pressure on our fighters to leave too.

It was a hard lesson to learn and one I had no intention of repeating. Our new Thai business partner is not from the MT fraternity and has a university degree obtained in Australia.

Som's departure from the business had no impact at all on customer acquisition. He had significantly overestimated his contribution to the business. It led us to realise that having a well-known Thai fighter as HT was not as crucial to our success as we presumed. This was a very important learning point for us. It gave us considerably more freedom when it came to recruiting trainer staff in the future.

Many foreigners are attracted to the MT business. MT camps are vibrant places to be. If you are at all competitively spirited, it ticks the boxes. The excitement runs high. My advice, however, to anyone considering in investing in a MT-related business would be to think carefully before partnering with someone whose life has been centred solely within that community. During the twelve years I have been here in Thailand I have seen countless foreigners investing in MT businesses and very few partnerships are successful. Many lose everything they've invested.

The majority of MT fighters come from impoverished families. In terms of their personal development, this has wider implications than just being poor. They lack role models and the communities they come from are not thriving. They are often taken away from their immediate families at a very young age, which can be nothing other than damaging emotionally. Educational opportunities are lacking, and many have little or no formal education after young adolescence. (Until relatively recently, students were not legally required to attend school after the age of 12.)

(The point about educational attainment is an important one to anyone considering a business relationship with a fighter brought up in one of these gyms. Although many gym owners these days place more importance on the education of the children they act in *loco parentis* for, this often was not the case in the past. Going into a business partnership with someone who missed very important years in their education means they will have a completely different frame of reference and understanding of what's required to make the business successful. Reconciling the different views is extremely challenging.)

Not only are fighters taken away from their families when they are young, they are then put in a rigid training environment where they are not required to make any real decisions for themselves. The gym owner decides everything: what they eat, when they sleep, their training regime, who they fight and when they fight. They have few choices to make of their own.

It's a harsh life, which they have little control over. As my first business partner once said to me, 'Fighting is not modelling, you know.' Even if they had been involved in the running of the gym they were brought up in, as explained elsewhere in the book, most traditional gyms were not operated as businesses. Additionally, the culture of doing business in a developing economy such as Thailand's is very different from that of developed/advanced economies of the West. All these factors mean that most MT fighters are operating from a different frame of reference to the one an investor might be more used to. Understandably, this creates enormous difficulties and tensions on both sides.

In the final analysis, I regard all these steps along the way as being an important part of the journey towards creating a successful business here in Thailand. I think about what happened often and how stressful it was but as they frequently say in the fight world, 'No pain, no gain'. I am philosophical about what happened because I learnt a lot along the way. It has allowed us to create a business which we feel proud of and are comfortable with. Our integrity is not compromised. For this I am immensely thankful.

Chapter 5
Building a Muay Thai Gym Team

Although most of my experience in employing Thai staff has been within the MT arena, many of the points raised here are applicable to recruitment generally in Thailand, especially if it is for non-professional staff.

Early in my career, I worked on a project with Hays Recruitment Consultants, still one of the global leaders in recruitment. They explained the importance of building networks as a significant number of job opportunities never reached the open marketplace. As far as landing the perfect job was concerned, the old adage 'It's not what you know but who you know' had a large part to play in success. This is most certainly the case in Thailand.

Within the MT community, in my experience, all staff are recruited via informal channels. If there are recruitment services in Thailand for non-professional positions, such as those we rely so heavily on in developed economies, I am not aware of them. This equally applies to contracting out services, such as building works, too.

In my early days at the gym I invested in, I suggested that we employ a building contractor other than the one usually used. I was told that in Thailand it's not wise to do this, as prior experience/knowledge was the only guarantee that the supplier was trustworthy. This both surprised and worried me. The longer I have been here, the more I understand this to be the case and the reasons why. Resources such as Trustpilot or Trading Standards are not commonplace here.

Traditionally, when MT gyms were largely community based, all the people training and working as trainers would have been well known, or often related to, the owner. These gyms were very close-knit communities and strong allegiances were formed within them, particularly amongst young fighters who often lived at the gym on a full-time basis. Similarly, close bonds were formed between trainers and the young fighters in their charge. They would often look after one another well after the fighter's career was over. Many of the older trainers employed at Sumalee over the years were trainers of our younger staff when they themselves were fighters. For young fighters, taken away from their families at an early age and often relocated to another part of the country, these bonds are long lasting and strong.

In these local-based community gyms, the trainers were effectively volunteers and were not employed in the conventional understanding of the term. If they lived at the gym, they would have been given accommodation and food in return for their services, but a regular salary would not have been part of the package. Financial remuneration would have come in the form of 'tips' taken out of gains from gambling or fight purses and given either by the gym owner or the fighter at their discretion. Arrangements such as these continue to the present day.

It was not unusual for young fighters to live at the gyms because their families were unable to look after them for some reason. In these situations, the gym owner acted in *loco parentis* although there was no legal foundation to the arrangement. The gym owner would take responsibility for living arrangements and education, as well as for their development as a fighter. He was responsible for organising their training and in complete control of their career by arranging suitable fight opportunities for them. Fighters, often failing to understand what their contribution to the equation was, felt a great debt of gratitude to the gym owner, who appeared to be magnanimous. Fighters were more often than not under contract, unable to extract themselves from this arrangement easily if at all.

Not only was there a feeling of indebtedness to the gym owner, the strong bonds formed between fighters and their trainers also engendered such emotions. Their life was very hard and they saw themselves as being in it all together. These bonds are so strong that loyalty is sometimes misdirected. As long as the status quo within the gym was not upset or their own relationships threatened, unacceptable and even criminal behaviour can be overlooked.

Even as the MT gym business has grown prolifically over the last decade, the majority of trainers are recruited to gyms because they know the Thai owner or have another connection at the gym. Nevertheless, the net is drawn wider than it was in the past. Although the system of patronage still exists, most contemporary gyms now operate a hybrid model of employing staff. Staff are still most likely to be drawn from a pool of people known either directly or indirectly but these gyms have transitioned to a more conventional employment model where staff are paid a fixed salary at the end of the month.

Nevertheless, although most trainers are now paid a regular monthly salary, they have little control over the terms of their employment or their working conditions. Many work without any formal or written employment contract. This means that the gym owner has a considerable degree of latitude in terms of how staff are treated. As significant numbers are not formally registered as employees under the social security system, they have no recourse under labour laws. It also means that they have no access to free healthcare, and should their employment be terminated for any reason, the social security system is not there to support them. This was why so many MT trainers suffered more hardship than was necessary from the ramifications of the Covid-19 pandemic on businesses. Many trainers lost their livelihoods when MT gyms were required to close for three months in 2020, at the start of the pandemic to contain the spread of the virus. Fighters and trainers alike were forced to return to their families in the countryside, as their gyms had no means of supporting them.

The way in which Thai staff are typically recruited to a gym places a foreigner coming in as an employer at a disadvantage. They have not formed these long-standing filial bonds which are often much stronger than any contractual employment obligation anyway. The absence of these bonds can result in significant issues when it comes to staff retention and the smooth running of the gym.

It also means that a foreigner entering into a business partnership with an established gym is likely to have an uphill struggle when it comes to forming meaningful relationships with the staff *in situ*. Existing staff are more likely than not to be related to or have a close association with the existing gym owner. In the event of any differences of opinion between the original owner and the new partner, Thai staff will always take the side of the former. This will happen regardless of the outcome for the business overall.

Very naively, I hadn't given this any thought before I went into the partnership at the first MT gym. As a woman, I suffered a further disadvantage when dealing with the trainer staff who were all male. Thai society is patriarchal but within the MT community, PATRIARCHY predominates without question.

Within a MT gym, men and women have very distinctive roles and usually there is no crossover. At the gym I invested in, I was very surprised when I heard laments that a male relative who was working as a cleaner also had to clean the toilets in the lodging rooms. I questioned why this was a problem as that was an essential part of the job. I was told that in Thailand, men do not clean toilets; this is regarded as the work of women. I was even more surprised that a female family member of the gym owner endorsed such ideas.

The first gym I was involved with adopted the hybrid model of employing staff. Almost all the staff were either related to the gym owner or had strong associations with him from his younger training/fighting days. He commanded a great deal of loyalty from them. During the time I was involved in the business, providing the member of staff had worked at the gym for at least three months, they were formally registered with the social security system. However, there was no formal or written contract of employment.

Foreigners who have considerable experience living and working in Thailand often claim it is not the Land of Smiles it appears to be. It was a considerable surprise to me at my previous gym that, although everything appeared to be glossy on the surface, it was a façade. Underlying divisions are not unique in any workplace, wherever you are in the world. In Thailand, where the culture of avoiding open confrontation or of being disrespectful is generally avoided, spotting what lies beneath the surface is more difficult. Even if you are in the midst of it yourself (as I have been at Sumalee), it can be difficult to see what's going on in front of you.

The more involved I became in the business, the more there was to see. It was difficult to comprehend that I had been unaware of it beforehand. Much of what I came to understand resulted from increased proficiency in the language and most particularly, Rhian's very swift acquisition of the language. For example, many of the trainers took advantage of the fact that the customers did not understand Thai language. They talked about and ridiculed them in their presence. This happens in a lot of gyms. When it was drawn to the existing owner's attention, he did try to tackle it. It was also something I had to address in the beginning at Sumalee.

The more trainers there are in a gym, then the more factions there are likely to be. These arise primarily from different allegiances built earlier in careers. It is difficult to spot but the rifts can be huge and can affect the ability of the business to grow. When I first joined the partnership, Rhian volunteered to give English lessons to the staff. A family member of the gym owner refused to sit in the presence of the gym's most popular trainer. There was no respect for him whatsoever even though he generated significant income for the gym. She abused her position as a close relative of the owner by being mean spirited to this trainer and his wife, who worked as a cleaner at the gym. As a close family member, she knew her position within the business was guaranteed regardless of how she behaved.

An example of this concerned the couple's young child. As a cleaner at the gym, the trainer's wife started work at 7am and the trainer started at 7.30am. Their son had to be taken to school at 7.45am. The relative refused to grant either of them the ten minutes required to take their child to school. No contract of employment meant they had no rights. As someone coming from a different employment environment I felt it necessary to intervene and allowed the wife the ten minutes required to take the child to school.

The relative later turned her wrath on me, using what I

now refer to as silent disobedience. This is where a member of staff, rather than discuss what their issue is, silently refuses to do anything you ask them to do. When you allocate the task, they will accept the request but simply ignore it later. This is a frequently used tactic in a culture where confrontation is avoided at all costs.

These underhand tactics are certainly not exclusive to Muay Thai gyms and come from a culture where saving face is everything. I briefly worked for a research company in Bangkok on a project where buyers of petroleum were interviewed. They were responsible for buying significant quantities. Their most frequent complaint was that, despite the fact they were customers, if they did anything to upset the supplier's staff, the service they received became poor.

In many respects, entering into the business I was involved in was like stepping back to Dickensian times. The relative's role was that of the mean-spirited Ebenezer. However, and in their defence, the person concerned adopted the role of protector of the business. The owner was often not present for one reason or another so the relative kept a careful eye on the business on his behalf.

It didn't take long for me to realise how isolated I was within the business. There was no meeting of minds and it certainly wasn't just about language. A business culture different to my own expectations and experience was operating there.

Sexual Harassment Claim

One of the incidents that opened my eyes was a complaint of sexual assault made by one of the students against a trainer. The reported incident happened outside of working hours and not on the gym's premises. The initial reaction was to terminate the employment of the trainer but it was not for the assault, it was because he didn't come to work the next day!

Two weeks later the trainer was back at work. When I asked why his employment had been reinstated, I was told that the claim was unsubstantiated and believed not to be true. This was despite the victim making a personal representation, explaining what had happened to her. Apparently, during the meeting, nothing was said to her and no apology or assistance was offered. The reaction probably stemmed from their being unused to such a direct approach, which resulted in a loss of face.

The incident demonstrated the strength of the bonds that existed and that had been built up over the years. The trainer in question had only a few months previously been found guilty in court of a violent assault on someone in a bar. Yet still the girl was not believed even though there was good reason to do so. They thought she was hysterical. Victim blaming is very common in Thailand and one British expat, Emma Thomas, has written extensively about her experience of being sexually assaulted at a MT gym, focusing on how she was treated by the gym owner and other members of the gym fraternity following the incident.

I would not like to leave the impression that sexual assaults in MT gyms in Thailand are widespread, but they do take place.

Women coming to train, live or work in Thailand should be aware of the culture when it comes to assaults on women and violence generally. The prevalence of domestic violence in Thailand was highlighted in an article in the *Bangkok Post*. It was reported here that in 2020 the Women and Men Progressive Movement Foundation monitored and collected data from ten newspapers between January and June and found 350 news articles involving domestic violence cases. Of the total articles collected, 57.4% of the cases were related to murder; 14.6% injuries; 10.9% suicide; 8.9% sexual violence by a family member; and 2.9% unintended pregnancies.

The notion of victim blaming in Thailand is a deep-rooted, multifaceted and endemic problem. The issue was brought into sharp focus when, after a rape and murder of a British tourist in 2014, Prime Minister Prayuth Chan-ocha made a controversial statement that sparked outrage worldwide: 'There are always problems with tourist safety,' he said. 'They think our country is beautiful and is safe so they can do whatever they want, they can wear bikinis and walk everywhere.' But, he added, 'Can they be safe in bikinis…unless they are not beautiful?'

The implication that attractive women in bikinis were not guaranteed safety in Thailand sparked immediate backlash. Although the Prime Minister apologised the next day, his apology raised further questions about the prevalence of victim blaming in Thai society.

'I am sorry with what I said and if it has caused any ill feelings,' he said, adding, 'I just wanted to warn tourists that we have different traditions and they have to stay on their toes.'

The statement begs an important question: which Thai traditions require women in bikinis to remain vigilant? To many in Thai society, the answer is threefold: patriarchy, rape culture and victim blaming.

The Prime Minister's public and inappropriate comments sparked the #DontTellMeHowToDress campaign, led by Thai model, actress and television host Cindy Bishop. Since that time victims of abuse – within a household, educational, employment or other setting – have been more likely to come forward to report their experiences to the public. There is now much more open discussion about this issue in the media and the topic is often covered.

Notwithstanding, there is a long way to go in a society where violence against women in a popular television series is an acceptable norm. Nevertheless, the conversation has now started, which will hopefully mean women in Thailand will be safer in the future.

Trainers who commit these offences are typically able to move freely from one gym to another because references neither exist nor are required. Sadly, because of fear of unpleasant and violent repercussions, the crimes are frequently not reported either to the police or to employers.

Being aware of this, Sylvie von Duuglas-Ittu, a long-term fighter in Thailand, has created a forum on her website, 8LimbsUs, where women can anonymously report any problem they have experienced, assisting others in identifying those gyms/trainers that are best to avoid.

Unknowingly, we employed a trainer who had been involved in such an incident at a gym whose owners we knew well. When we employed the trainer, we had no idea why his previous gym had let him go and they did not inform us. As soon as we found out, we asked him to leave. There needs to be more co-operation among gyms generally and especially concerning matters such as these to prevent perpetrators moving from one gym to another with impunity.

Generally speaking, I have noticed that many Thai fighters behave like adolescents in their interactions with the opposite sex. More likely than not, this stems from being closeted away for a lengthy period during their formative years in a predominantly male environment, which results in both immature and irresponsible behaviour towards women.

The sexual assault incident at the gym I invested in was just the tip of the iceberg. The cultural differences in thinking and approach were so wide they could not be bridged. I felt I could no longer, with integrity, remain within that business. The huge chasm between my business partner and I in terms of our education, experience and culture meant that unfortunately we could not work together. To this day, I think the outcome was regrettable because if working together had been possible, I believe the synergy of his background as a highly acclaimed fighter and mine in business would have ultimately created something truly impressive. Sadly, circumstances did not allow this to happen.

Hierarchy in the Gym

A MT gym is a delicate 'eco-system' and if the balance is tipped in the wrong direction, interpersonal relationships within the gym can deteriorate quickly. There is a clear but unwritten rule set that determines hierarchical order within the gym. The working environment, especially in a traditional gym, is made up of a close-knit community where often trainers and students live and work together on a full-time basis. When important fights are on the horizon, they are operating under a great deal of pressure. The training is harsh, frequently involving weight cuts for fighters, and so fuses are short. It's the unwritten hierarchy within the gym that keeps everything in order.

The most important factor that defines order in the gym is age. I wrote about this in a blog post published on our website some years ago. Simply put, the older a person is the more respect they command. However, gender does create exceptions to this rule.

Generally speaking, women have the lowest status within the gym hierarchy. In more westernised gyms, this may be less obvious but in Thailand gender stereotypes are deeply rooted. Sylvie von Duuglas-Ittu, who has written extensively about her experiences of training in Thailand, has a number of articles on this topic on her website 8LimbsUs.

Given this misogyny, the question as to how a woman managed to build a successful gym like Sumalee may well be asked. As always there are exceptions to these cultural norms. Being the eldest person in our gym gave me enormous leverage. I was 56 when we opened Sumalee Boxing Gym. Had I have been younger, I believe my path to success would have been more difficult, if not impossible. Another important determinant of position within the social hierarchy in Thailand is perceived 'power'. 'Power' in Thailand relates to occupation/position and very importantly, perceived financial strength. As owner of the gym, I scored highly on these parameters. This supposed power also served me well within the wider misogynous MT community.

Having a clear understanding of the social dynamics within a gym structure is of course important. In addition, an understanding as to how to establish a reputable training facility is also vital if a MT gym business is to be successful.

Most traditional MT gyms have one or more well-known fighters associated with them, whether past or present. Usually they have trained these fighters from a young age and brought them to at least Bangkok stadium level. This gives the gym status and prestige within the wider fight community and credibility as a training institution.

To meet the burgeoning demand created by international fighters/students, many of the gyms catering for this influx are foreign owned/backed. For them to establish their credibility, they either partner with a well-known fighter or place a well-known fighter at the head of the trainer team. Unfortunately, this can place the gym owner in a precarious position as we found on the two occasions that we took this path. Our experience with HTs is not an unusual one for foreign gym owners.

The majority of well-known retired fighters do not originate from commercial gyms. In traditional MT gyms, most of the income is derived from either the fight purse or, more importantly, gambling. In a commercial MT gym, especially a foreign-owned gym, income from these sources is usually negligible with the gym being primarily reliant on the external customers for survival. Understanding this gave us confidence. It has been the key to our success both in building the business and in overcoming the problems associated with being dependent on well-known MT personalities.

The explosion in demand for MT training created by people travelling from overseas has been underpinned by the growth in smartphone ownership. Simply put, nowadays more people worldwide know about the existence of MT gyms and the possibility that anybody can come and train in them. Not only is there more information available, it is available in English too. MT gyms are no longer the domain of elite fighters. The most successful MT gyms are those that understand the importance of digital marketing, brand building and market positioning, and can cater to the needs of foreign tourists and holidaymakers.

Bearing in mind the educational experience and attainment of most MT fighters, the shift in focus and how success is achieved are not understood. Both of our previous HTs did not appreciate the softer skills involved in building a business and quickly assumed they had a greater importance in attracting students than was actually the case. The first HT in particular became overly influenced by the people around him who themselves didn't understand even basic principles of building a business.

As we did not have connections within the MT fraternity

ourselves, most of our trainers were recruited through the HTs. What developed in the gym in the early years was a similar situation to the one I found at the gym I invested in. That is, all the trainers had a far greater affiliation to the HT than they did to either the business or myself. Each HT, therefore, had a considerable amount of influence on the other training staff.

What happened in our gym commonly happens in foreign-owned gyms. The HT begins to believe that students come to the gym specifically to train with them. As the business grows, their assumed importance grows. Having no understanding as to how long it takes to build a business, they demand more and more. If they don't get what they want, their performance deteriorates. This in itself is a problem but it's their influence on the other trainers, who feel indebted to them, which exacerbates the problem significantly.

Alcohol and drug abuse is also a well-known problem within the Thai fighter community and many have written about their experiences and observations. The HT acts as a role model to the other trainers. Once the HT's behaviour and demeanour deteriorate, so do those of the other trainers.

The complexity of relationships within the gym, as previously described, makes addressing such problems challenging. In Thai culture, confrontation is avoided. To avoid generating feelings of *noi jai* (being offended or slighted), an indirect approach is needed. Approaching things in the wrong way results in a difficult-to-breach stonewall. At this stage, communication breaks down.

In the case of both of our past HTs, the situation in the gym had become critical and impossible to ignore. The level of service and training provided to our customers was being significantly prejudiced. Trainers were arriving late for work, often hungover or worse, still intoxicated. There were also factions in the gym with rivalries among trainers.

When we were unable to resolve our differences in a meaningful way, I had no option other than to terminate their employment, each in their turn. The first, who was overly subject to outside influences, was asked to leave. The second was dismissed without notice because of inappropriate behaviour towards a customer.

The first HT used his influence on the other training staff by taking most of them with him when he left. The second HT tried to do the same but was less successful.

Our experiences with these HTs and others described in other chapters of the book, made it abundantly clear that the traditional way of staffing the trainer team was not going to work for us. We started a programme of change immediately.

The priority was to alter the way we recruited and retained our trainer staff. Although it was still necessary to recruit via our existing trainer base, we started casting the net much wider and made sure the trainers came from different sources. We no longer have a designated HT role. Our General Manager, who was recruited from outside the MT community, oversees our trainer staff. He previously worked at one of the leading hotel brands on the island. He has had considerable training in customer service and understands the importance of this. He is older than all the trainer staff and, in line with the order in Thai culture, commands respect because of this.

We had always made sure our trainers were registered in the social security system. We introduced mutually binding employment contracts, which gave the trainers more rights (such as paternity leave, holiday entitlement, housing expenses, travel expenses, annual salary increases) and clearly stipulated their roles and responsibilities. It is an unusual but positive change to introduce employment contracts into a Muay Thai gym business in Thailand.

To improve staff retention, all trainers are given one

month's salary as a bonus for each year they stayed with us. Where the opportunities for career progression are limited, together with the Buddhist philosophy of living in the present moment, motivating staff is challenging. We have found that the annual financial bonus has significantly reduced staff turnover.

In recent years opportunities for MT trainers to work overseas, especially in China, have increased. Consequently, all MT gyms will need to take a serious look at ways of preventing their staff from being enticed by higher salaries to work overseas.

It took us a long time to figure out what was the best way of fusing our employment norms and expectations with the established norms within the MT community. It was often stressful and sometimes emotionally painful. Having found a way that works for us, we have established an excellent team of trainers. They are the backbone of the MT side of our business and we now have a team that work together for the benefit of the business and the customers. The atmosphere in the gym has changed beyond recognition, producing a much happier working environment.

Irrespective of any other skills we have brought to the business, it is my strong belief that growth would not have been possible without some fluency in Thai language. Although we have tried to teach them and despite their level of contact with English-speaking guests, most of our Thai staff are reluctant to fully embrace another language. I was blessed in that Rhian learnt to speak, read and write Thai quickly. This meant I always had someone whom I could trust to act on my behalf in communicating with the Thai staff. Although nowhere near Rhian's level of proficiency, my own fluency has grown over the years. I am currently learning to read and write Thai too. Any entrepreneur who tries to build a business in Thailand without a preparedness to learn the language is inviting a rocky ride.

Migrant Workers

Migrant workers are defined as people who leave their home country to work in another country. They do not usually have the intention to stay permanently in the country in which they work.

In Thailand, migrant workers predominantly come from Burma or developed economies such as Europe, USA, Australia, Russia and China.

We have employed many Burmese staff at Sumalee and they have been an essential part of the workforce. Obtaining permits for Burmese staff to legally work in Thailand is a relatively straightforward and inexpensive process. All our housekeepers and kitchen staff are Burmese. We have found the work ethic of Burmese employees to be such that the small additional cost of obtaining work permits for them is well worth it. They have been loyal, hardworking and reliable. Many Burmese also speak some English and those who have been here for a long time often speak Thai as well, although they cannot read it. We have had staff who only speak Burmese, some who speak Burmese and English, and others who speak Burmese and Thai. Within the business, many of us communicate with one another through a third person, which adds an interesting dimension to the day.

Compared with employing Burmese, employing people from non-Asean countries involves considerably more administration and expense. It is illegal for a foreigner to work in Thailand without a work permit, howsoever that work is defined. Even volunteers should have a work permit. There is a list of jobs which foreigners are not allowed to do as they are protected for Thai workers.

For a company to obtain a work permit, it needs to have a defined amount of paid up share capital, the amount depending on how many work permits are required. The company must be registered for VAT in order to qualify. Per work permit and working visa which qualifies an employee to stay in the country for one year without needing to exit, the company must have at least four Thai staff, all whom must be registered to pay monthly social security. Migrant workers from non-Asean countries are entitled to a minimum wage, and personal tax is payable on this. The company that sponsors the employee is responsible for paying this tax.

These requirements and duties are not unusual and are comparable to employing foreign workers in other countries. In a MT business such as a training camp where the income stream is variable and seasonally dependent, the expenses involved can be prohibitive. This in turn can inhibit growth of the business. On an island such as Phuket, accessing suitably qualified local staff is not always possible. This is something entrepreneurs need to bear in mind when investing in Thailand.

Chapter 6
The Signing of Saenchai

Many of you reading this might not be from the MT world and may be wondering who Saenchai is. If you haven't heard of him, he is probably the most internationally well-known MT fighter of all time.

> Saenchai (*born July 30, 1980*), formerly known as Saenchai Sor. Kingstar is a Thai Muay Thai fighter. Saenchai won the Lumpini Stadium title, which is widely considered the most prestigious title in Muay Thai, in four different weight divisions, while mostly fighting larger opponents. He is considered by many to be the best pound for pound Muay Thai fighter, and is regarded as one of the best fighters of all time. Saenchai would often give up weight to find worthy opponents in Thailand, and from 2003-2014 only lost two times in Thailand when the weights were equal, with all other losses happening when he was forced to have a weight disadvantage to make the fights more evenly matched. Against foreigners the gap in skill is so great he will go up as high as 147 pounds, which is 15+ pounds above his optimal weight class. (Source: Wikipedia)

In my opinion, accessibility to the superstars of the sport is one of the reasons MT is so popular internationally, especially amongst young people. It's possible to really get involved. Many followers will have seen Saenchai fight and may even have met him personally. In common with many other MT superstars, he is personable and makes himself accessible. He is always ready for a photo opportunity and to sign his autograph.

Accessibility pertains also to the cost of purchasing a MT fighter's contract, should it be available. In the world of MT, Saenchai is effectively the equivalent in career and accomplishment to the best top league football players. It is unimaginable that a person like me could have any intervention whatsoever in a professional football player's career, at any level at all.

Lack of investment in the national sport of Thailand is a huge issue that has ramifications right down the line. In a recent article in *Asean Today*, based on the Global Wealth Report published by Credit Suisse in 2018, Thailand was highlighted to have the largest wealth gap in the world. One per cent of the population in Thailand controls over 67% of the wealth. Five hundred people own 36% of the equity in all Thailand's firms, according to the Bank of Thailand. Sadly, it is possible that lack of investment in MT is a reflection of the overall low regard in which the sport is held within the upper echelons of Thai society.

Nevertheless, the last ten years have seen a burgeoning of international interest in the sport. Until then, most of the superstars were only well-known within Thailand itself. This was because, unless you have lived or trained in Thailand, much of what went on here remained within the domain of the country. There was little information available in English and indeed an overall paucity of digital footprint. Any video material that existed from before 2008 was largely taken or owned by a Thai TV channel.

Although YouTube came into existence in 2005, until smartphones became widely available, its use was not commonplace. This was true of all the social media channels that gained real traction only once smartphone ownership was widespread. Apple launched the iPhone in 2007. Smartphones changed how people used social media, giving it more immediacy because people were able to access the internet on the move.

In the early millennium, interest in MT outside Thailand had been growing but interest escalated considerably when the growth of social media channels converged with the growth in smartphone ownership. The smartphone was not only a tool to enable people to record the moment; it facilitated access to the internet too. The time when the two came together marked a huge change in the MT 'industry'. More gyms catering for the Western market opened up, primarily in areas that attracted large numbers of tourists such as Bangkok, Pattaya, Phuket and Koh Samui.

What was most interesting was how this resulted in a sea change of opportunity for the more accomplished MT fighters. Almost overnight, a number of them became international brands. Saenchai was one of these fighters who was in the right place at the right time.

By 2010 Saenchai was 30 years old and had nearly finished his mainstream career in Thailand, primarily fighting at the two main stadiums in Bangkok (Rajadamnern and Lumpinee) for stadium belts. Prior to 2010, he had only ever had four fights outside Asia. However, in the decade between 2010 and January 2020, due to the rise in international exposure, Saenchai had eighty-eight fights overseas in fifteen countries.

I was lucky enough to be involved in Saenchai's career

for a short period in 2010/2011 when he was on the cusp of moving from a career largely based in Thailand to becoming an international superstar.

When I invested in the gym in Nai Harn, Phuket, the finances and business acumen I brought meant things started to change quickly. At the outset of my involvement in the gym, there was one customer staying there. Within three months, we were turning people away. As well as contributing to the improvement of the marketing and putting in place better systems/processes for dealing with enquiries and bookings, my financial investment meant the gym could buy the contract of well-known fighters such as Saenchai. Without my investment this would not have been possible. With it, the fortunes of the gym changed completely.

Saenchai had been released from his contract with the gym that sponsored him throughout the majority of his early career. He was a free agent. He needed to improve his circumstances and he was looking for a gym to buy him. He knew that if he could find a suitable gym, he would be able to keep all the proceeds from the purchase as he was accountable to no one but himself at that time.

More established gyms would not have been interested in a purchase like Saenchai. Their focus at the time was within Thailand and they were looking for new blood. Fighters who could earn their keep whilst at the same time build the reputation of the gym as a place of excellence for training. Saenchai's career was beyond that and to acquire him required (in Thai terms) a substantial amount of money. As the international market for fighters like Saenchai was only just beginning to grow, he probably would have been viewed as well past his sell-by date.

My business partner was a similar age to Saenchai and of the same generation of fighters. The MT community then was particularly close-knit as it was largely based within Thailand, primarily in Bangkok. My business partner knew him and became aware that Saenchai was looking for a new gym to base himself.

My business partner and I had a long discussion about the pros and cons of taking Saenchai on, as we knew that ownership would be in name only. We were worried that in reality the amount of time Saenchai would actually spend at the gym would be very limited, perhaps reducing the value of the investment. As it turned out, Saenchai proved to be a valuable investment for the gym itself, although not for me personally. Little did I know at the time but I was effectively signing my own exit card when we bought him!

Saenchai, quite rightly by that stage in his career, was able to call the tune to a large extent. Nevertheless, he had a need at the time and so did our gym in Nai Harn, which had been running with only short bursts of profitability for over five years by that time. We needed to grow the business and we figured that, at the right price, purchasing Saenchai was well worth the risk. One thing that my business partner and I did have in common was that taking on new challenges got our adrenaline going. We agreed between us a budget of what we were prepared to pay. The money for the purchase was to come out of our own pockets and not from the business, paying 50% each.

My business partner approached Saenchai and said we were interested in making an offer. Rather than telling Saenchai what our offer was, the Thai way is to ask the recipient what amount would satisfy him. We were astounded that Saenchai said he wanted THB500,000 (at the time £10,000), which in fact was well below our budget.

Subsequently, when Saenchai had given more thought to his situation, he changed his mind and asked for

THB600,000. This was still within budget but my business partner told Saenchai that he would have to ask me personally during an impending trip to Bangkok that we had already planned.

The trip was to attend the first ever Thai Fight quarter finals, held on 25 October 2010. This was a massive occasion, staged in the National Stadium, Rajamangala, in Bangkok. Without a doubt, Thai Fight has played a huge part in widening the appeal of MT both within and outside Thailand. Prior to professionally presented shows like this, Thais saw MT as something rather dingy. Thai Fight changed all of that.

It was as near to a rock concert as you could possibly get, without it actually being a concert. The capacity of the stadium is 50,000 and it looked to be near-full capacity. The audience was primarily Thai, coming from all walks of life and in stark contrast to the audience traditionally associated with the more established Bangkok stadiums. I was buzzing following this show as it gave me an indication of the potential MT had in terms of popular appeal.

Incidentally, Liam Harrison (at that time a well-known, accomplished and active fighter from the UK) fought in this show against the Japanese fighter Soichiro Miyakoshi. It was the first and only time I saw him fight. As a UK national, I was particularly interested to watch him. At the peak of his career at the time, he won the fight but was disqualified as he came in over the maximum weight of 67kg. Miyakoshi took his place in the semi-finals.

The 2010 tournament was eventually won by Fabio Pinca (France), who fought Youseff Boughanen (Belgium) on 6 December 2010 in Nakhon Ratchasima, Thailand.

We met Saenchai on the morning before the Thai Fight promotion at our hotel. Looking back, and bearing in mind his rapid rise to international fame, it is incredible to remember how nervous he was to ask me for the extra THB100,000 (£2,000 at the time). He had picked up a serviette from the table, which he was twisting around nervously like a set of worry beads! He politely asked me directly if it would be possible to increase the payment for him to THB600,000. We teased him somewhat and told him we would have to give it due consideration. We informed him about a week later that we accepted the increase.

We made the announcement that Saenchai would be joining the gym around 5 November 2010. This was around the start of the tourism high season, although the timing of the announcement was not planned for this reason. The interest in this acquisition was extraordinary as was the sudden surge in demand to train at the gym. The bookings flowed in and turnover doubled in December. By January 2011, turnover had trebled. Initially it felt like a buoyant and exciting time for me.

Saenchai's arrival at the gym was regarded as of sufficient local importance that the Mayor of Rawai and his team welcomed him personally. His feelings at the time were recorded in an interview by Mike LNg on thescienceof8limbs website, which Rhian assisted in providing the translation for. In the interview he emphasised that the move was stimulated by wanting to improve the lifestyle circumstances of his family: 'I wanted to change my lifestyle and have a better life for me and my family. I wanted a more relaxed lifestyle. I wanted a better life for my wife and my son who is now 9 years old.'

Sadly, behind the scenes, there was a lot going on. Once Saenchai joined the gym and turnover quickly escalated, the huge strains between myself and my business partner exacerbated and his perceived need for a business partner was dramatically reduced. I began the three-month process of exiting the business in March 2011 but in reality, the breakdown in the business relationship started in December 2010, only four months after I joined.

Nevertheless, I did have the pleasure of working with Saenchai for several months after he joined the gym. In all honesty, he was a pleasure to work with and his deep love of and expertise in MT were clear. He worked tirelessly to encourage his students to do well and he is a true champion of the sport.

Not long after he joined the gym, we held a workshop led by him. It sold out and we accepted about forty students to attend. Saenchai sparred with every one of those who wanted to take the opportunity to do so. He took a great deal of care to match the level of sparring with the ability of each individual student. One student did try to take advantage of his good nature to gain the better of him. He regretted it, as Saenchai was quick to change his pace. He said he was tired beyond belief but would not deny anyone the opportunity if they wanted to spar with him despite this.

I had the honour of promoting two shows with Saenchai on the card. I believe I would be correct in saying that no other foreign woman has even had this privilege in Thailand. In one of the shows, Saiyok Pumpanmuang was also on the fight card. In both cases, the shows held in Bangla Boxing Stadium, Patong, were a sellout even though they were show fights. They were also the only shows promoted during my time at the gym that made a profit. Unfortunately, the profit made on the shows featuring Saenchai was outweighed by the losses made on the other shows we promoted. (Chapter 9 explains the economics of show promotions.)

Saenchai stayed at the gym in Nai Harn for approximately eighteen months. During that time, he fought outside Thailand at least seven times (UK, Australia, Japan, USA, Milan, Paris and China). The period marks his move towards an international career where he usually took on heavier foreign fighters. His only ever loss to a foreign fighter during this period was when he fought Fabio Pinca in Milan in January 2012.

During my own time as his owner/manager, Saenchai fought one of his foreign favourites, Liam Harrison, in Doncaster in the UK. He won the fight and received a fight purse of around £5,000. Of this, he retained £3,000, and my business partner and I received £1,000 each (THB50,000 at the time).

When I left the gym, my business partner bought me out of my ownership of Saenchai. Unless I wanted to make life difficult for myself, I had no real choice in this matter. I understand Saenchai left the gym in Nai Harn soon after over differences of opinion regarding a loss. He was able to buy himself out of his contract and left to join PK Saenchai Gym.

Saenchai is a true legend. I have met him many times since I parted company with the gym in Nai Harn, usually at Thai Fight shows, which he was contracted to for many years. Indeed, he fought one of the Scottish fighters sponsored by Sumalee Boxing Gym in a Thai Fight promotion in Vietnam. Unfortunately, it was not a good performance from our fighter who was diminished by the experience. He also suffered a good deal of public derision from notable fighters within the UK MT community regarding his performance against Saenchai. This was bad sportsmanship and sadly reflects the lack of professionalism by many foreigners involved in the sport.

Saenchai is always polite and respectful when we meet. My short involvement in his career, was incredibly satisfying and certainly a highlight of my involvement in the MT business. One thing for sure, after we brought him to the gym, the number of people training there increased dramatically. The ripple effect of his influence on the volume of customers training at the gym lasted a long time after he had left.

Chapter 7
Sponsoring Muay Thai Fighters

Despite being in Thailand for twelve years, and during all that time being involved in the MT business, I cannot claim to know everything about how the MT business operates here. The situation is ever changing and complex. The best I can do is relate situations I have encountered and my understanding of contemporary MT.

To set the scene, it is important to understand that MT gyms traditionally were not run as commercial operations. They did not derive their income from people coming to train on a drop-in basis or from overseas visitors staying in accommodations provided by the gym. All commercial gyms are therefore an adaption of the traditional gym model.

Traditionally, most MT gyms were local village gyms. They provided a focus for the community and a place where young boys in particular could learn MT skills and compete. Some even acted as an informal orphanage, providing a needed service to the community. The gym would provide an option for parents who were, for whatever reason, unable to care for their sons (mainly). The parents could take their child to a gym and the gym owner would look after them. In return, the child was expected to help around the gym (cleaning, preparing food, etc.), train and, more often than not, fight at local shows.

Sometimes the gym owners were benefactors and used their personal resources to help support the children. In other gyms, the fight purses were used to contribute to the upbringing and welfare of the children. Responsible gym owners took good care of the children and ensured they were educated. Fighters of the golden age of MT (early 1980s to mid-1990s), though, were unlikely to have received a full education beyond the age of around 12. In those days, education beyond the age of 12 was not compulsory in Thailand.

If the fighter was good enough, he might have been sent on to one of the well-known gyms in Bangkok to benefit from a higher level of training and appropriate training partners. It also provided them with easier access to the two main stadiums to compete: Lumpinee and Rajadamnern. Other skilled fighters travelled back and forth to Bangkok from their hometowns. Many were from Esaan and the journey time could be four to six hours each way. Wherever they were based, the training regimes were harsh and the fight programmes in Bangkok made school attendance intermittent at best and impossible at worst. There are fewer village gyms these days although many still exist. Conditions and educational attainment tend to be better than was the case in the past.

Fight purses from local matchups even today are small, perhaps not more than THB1,000 to THB2,000 for the youngest children. Children will often have their first fight at around six years of age. To have access to more lucrative fight purses, fighters need to be fighting in the big shows in Bangkok. The range of options for shows has increased greatly in the last ten years or so. Lumpinee and Rajadamnern have always been the Holy Grail for MT fighters. These stadiums offer a league table based on excellence and to get to the top in any weight category is hugely meritorious. Until the last five or so years it was hard for foreign fighters to be competing in the leagues in these stadiums. It was even rarer for a foreign fighter to become a stadium champion within any of the weight categories. The shows at these stadiums are subsidised by ticket sales to foreigners, and consequently fight purses, once the fighter becomes known, are much higher.

Most foreign fighters with a matchup at Lumpinee earn less than THB10,000, which is lower than they would earn on shows such as Max Muay Thai and Thai Fight (see Chapter 9). Because of the perceived prestige of fighting at these stadiums, fighters are prepared to accept lower fight purses solely for the opportunity of being there.

Technically, the fight purse belongs to the fighter. Thai fighters will have a contract with their gym that specifies how the purse will be divided between the gym and the fighter. The Sports Authority officially regulates the contracts but in reality, the gym decides what happens. This varies considerably from gym to gym. There are no rules for foreign fighters governing this. Some foreign fighters who become popular with the promoters are able to do well out of their fight career but many others struggle.

Thai fighters are registered by their gym with the Sports Authority. If they are not registered with the Sports Authority they cannot fight at Lumpinee or Rajadamnern. Thai fighters are retained by their gym under contract. These contracts are very restrictive. In many cases, gyms will not release the fighters from their contract. They seek a return for any investment they have made in training and taking care of living expenses. Some gyms are prepared to ruin a discontented fighter's career rather than release them from a contract (see Chapter 8).

Sponsored Foreign Fighters

The new wave of MT gyms catering for the foreign/tourist market started early in the millennium and were based on the traditional model of a MT gym. This meant they needed fighters. Since they were neither well-established nor based in a local community, the ready supply of local Thai youngsters was not available to them. They were also primarily located in established tourist hubs such as Phuket, Koh Samui, Koh Phang Ngan and Chiang Mai. These areas are more prosperous than the poor rural areas where MT gyms are usually located. In consequence, the role of providing a refuge for poor local children was mostly redundant for the new wave of gyms.

However, the new wave of gyms have available to them a pool of foreign fighters who are hugely keen to have the opportunity to live and train in Thailand. To promote themselves and showcase their training skills, many gyms sponsor foreign fighters. Most of these foreign fighters would not have been able to have a career in fighting without sponsorship support from the new wave of commercial gyms.

Sumalee started sponsoring foreign fighters as soon as we opened in December 2011. It was a mutually beneficial arrangement. It provided the gym with content for online promotion and it enabled the fighter to fulfil their dream of living and training in Thailand. All the fighters we fully sponsored and many of those who were partially sponsored received significant benefit in terms of the advancement of their careers as a result. Not least, they benefitted from the tutelage of much more experienced practitioners of the sport at no cost to themselves.

With increased tenure at Sumalee, they found more opportunities and became better known and respected as fighters, notching up considerable experience in the early stages of their professional careers. Many have subsequently used this experience and knowledge to set themselves up as trainers and work in gyms all over the world. In parallel, the variety of shows available to foreign fighters increased significantly since we opened in 2011.

Our fighters appeared in numerous well-known promotions throughout Thailand, such as Thai Fight, Max Muay Thai, MX Extreme, Toyota Cup, Top King, Izuzu Cup, King's Cup, Queen's Cup and Lumpini. We also took fighters to many different parts of Thailand and other places, including the UK, USA, Panama, Vietnam, Hong Kong, China and Malaysia.

The fighters we sponsored fell into two broad categories. Some received considerable support from their families. In these cases, the gym had a good deal of contact with the families involved and broadly speaking, the sponsorship experience was more rewarding for all concerned. For others, the amount of help they received from their families was negligible. This meant they were constantly under financial stress and life was tremendously tough for them. Realistically it was not possible for them to derive income in other ways because their training regime was intense and regulations regarding foreigners working in Thailand are strict. It was this group of fighters who were more difficult to manage and the outcome was considerably less satisfactory.

The level of sponsorship we gave to some of the fighters went well beyond what they would have been able to obtain from most other gyms. A breakdown of deductions made from the fight purse of two of the fighters is given below for illustrative purposes. This gives an indication of the direct financial return Sumalee received from the fighters.

Examples of those who received full sponsorship for a prolonged period were:

Central American Woman (one-year full sponsorship)

– she approached me after the closure of the gym in Phuket where she was training. She and her partner were given full sponsorship, which included a room at the gym and full access to training as well as fight apparel. She fought for us approximately thirteen times. The only deduction from her fight purse was THB500 occasionally taken as a contribution to oil, handwraps etc. for her fight.

Central American Man (one-year full sponsorship) – although retired from fighting himself, this fighter received sponsorship alongside his partner (above). He shared a room at the gym with his partner and had full access to training. He fought three times. His deductions were as above. He helped as a trainer for a few months for which he was paid.

Scottish Man (three years) – this fighter approached us requesting sponsorship after meeting at an event in Malaysia. He received full sponsorship including accommodation outside the gym and full access to training. He fought for us approximately thirty-one times. (He arranged one or two fights for himself in the UK during the time he trained with us.) Of the fights arranged by us, deductions were only taken from fights where his fight purse exceeded THB10,000. This happened on approximately eight occasions. Other than this, he retained his full fight purse and all training, accommodation, apparel and expenses were covered by Sumalee.

Scottish Man (two and a half years) – invited by us to receive full sponsorship, initially for a year, which was subsequently extended.

English Man (two years) – a contact in the UK approached us and asked us to give this fighter the opportunity of training in Thailand. He was given full sponsorship initially for three months, which was extended on an ongoing basis for nearly two and a half years.

English Man (one year) – full sponsorship including on-site accommodation with air conditioning and full access to training.

All these fighters and others received considerable support from the gym including: fight clothing supplied by Sumalee and Ultim8; equipment from Sandee Thailand; all transport to fights was arranged and only when the fight purse was over THB10,000 was the fighter asked to contribute to transportation costs; the support of a fight team, usually two trainers (the trainers were paid a salary so fighters were not obliged to tip them when their fight purse was low, which it usually was); and full media support including fight photos and good quality videos uploaded for posterity to our YouTube channel. In cases where the fighter received little support outside of that provided by Sumalee, we assisted by: obtaining sponsorship for them from some of our customers; ensuring they were fed; giving them professional advice on nutrition and reducing the price of meal plans available to them. In one case, we even helped by purchasing their visa.

It is very unusual for a gym to help a sponsored fighter with the cost of their visa. The fighter in question had been with us for a couple of years. He had always been in the shadow of a couple of other fighters we had training with us at the time. It appeared, however, that he was on the cusp of a breakthrough and had been selected by promoters to appear in some well-known promotions. This particular fighter received little external funding. His visa was due for renewal and he was unable to finance it himself. I sympathised with his position and offered for the gym to pay for a one-year visa for him. We purchased the visa in October and by February he left our gym to join a competitor gym without good reason or giving notice. Needless to add, neither he nor the gym he went to reimbursed us for what was outstanding on his visa.

Many of our customers were extremely generous with

the sponsored fighters and helped them in different ways. Sometimes this help was simply by treating them to a meal. One customer bought the fighters a fridge for their room to enable them to keep food fresh. Another sponsored a fighter's meal plan (breakfast and dinner every day) for three months. Two of our customers even fully sponsored a trip to Nepal/Everest for one of our fighters.

Since Sumalee opened in 2011, and as of this writing, we have sponsored fully or partially at least twenty-five foreign fighters and numerous Thai fighters. Fighters sponsored represented the following countries: Thailand, United Kingdom, USA, Mexico, Costa Rica, Australia, Cyprus, Ecuador and Egypt.

Throughout the course of their sponsorship by the gym, all Sumalee fighters were provided with the backup of a media service funded by the gym. We kept a full digital record of their sponsorship through videos of their fights, other video material, high-quality photos and often blog posts too. This gave them, and still does, considerable exposure. Mike Davis, who worked for us as media manager during our busiest sponsorship period, created a solid digital footprint from which we have been able to grow. Our followers on social media number far higher than those of any of the individual fighters we sponsored, and our YouTube channel has just over 40,000 subscribers at the time of writing.

The fight career of most fighters in Thailand, particularly foreign fighters, is usually short-lived for a number of reasons. Many simply do not make the grade. Some only become fighters to give themselves a means of staying in Thailand for a prolonged period. In consequence, they do not have the dedication needed to succeed. There is no established career pathway for a foreign fighter in Thailand. It's therefore easy for even the most skilled and committed fighters to lose interest or motivation. Maintaining discipline takes a lot of focus, and the wear and tear on the body is great. Added to this is the poor financial return that can result in considerable hardship for the fighter. On realising that a long-term career in the sport is not viable, many choose to carve out a career as a trainer. Our library of video and photographic material is used once they have left Sumalee as a resource for the fighter to promote themselves.

The impermanence of foreign fighters is a key factor to bear in mind when it comes to building the business. It is neither possible nor desirable to build the reputation of a gym around a sponsored foreign fighter. At most, they should form part of the marketing mix.

Sumalee had written contracts with most of our fighters, which they were required to sign and adhere to. Unlike the contracts issued to Thai fighters, however, these contracts are difficult to enforce on either a short- or long-term basis. The contracts are not legally binding. This effectively means sponsored fighters can come and go as they please. And they did! It frequently happened that trainers would put a lot of effort into a fighter only to find their leaving with short notice (or even with no notice at all). Sometimes they would return to their home country. All too often, they were poached by another gym (a pervading problem experienced by Thai gyms as well as foreign-owned gyms). Others gained the impression they'd get a better sponsorship deal/opportunity elsewhere. With regard to the sponsored fighters, nothing was permanent and the gym certainly had no guarantee there would be any return at all for the effort put into training and promoting the fighter.

In reality, the contracts were of use solely to outline a code of conduct that fighters were expected to adhere to. These contracts covered a number of broad areas with guidelines on:

- Training regime
- Fight purses
- Behaviour in the gym
- Behaviour towards staff
- Use of social media
- Interaction with the customers
- Illegal substance abuse

The majority of our fighters adhered to these guidelines, were hard working and were committed to training and fighting. They were disciplined, respectful and understood the order of a Thai gym. Readers should know we had some positive experiences and outcomes with some of our sponsored fighters.

Fight Purses

A fighter based in Thailand long term, tends to be much better matched for their fights as the promoter gets to know them and their skill level. Those who show talent and flair become favourites of the promoters. Skilled and entertaining fighters are in demand because they attract an audience. Promoters have complete control when it comes to getting fight opportunities. If either the gym or the fighter upsets a promoter, forthcoming fight opportunities are likely to be limited.

The promoter also decides what the fight purse will be. Until the fighter is known, successful and in demand for promotions, in general the fight purse is low. Even when a fighter is more established, the fight purse is hardly enough for the fighter to make a reasonable living out of fighting. Typically, a fighter competes only once a month. If they get injured, this can result in months out of the game with no income.

If fighters compete in local shows in rural areas of Thailand, the earnings may be as little as THB1,000 to THB2,000. This is why few of them do it. In tourist areas, where shows are put on for the benefit of visiting tourists, who pay handsomely for their tickets, the fight purse is higher. At Bangla and Patong stadiums in Phuket, once a fighter is known, women will receive a purse of THB6,000 and men THB6,000 to THB10,000. Ten thousand baht is very much at the upper end of the scale in stadiums such as these and a foreign fighter must be renowned to receive this amount.

Sumalee's fully sponsored fighters were given their entire fight purse earned in Bangla and Patong Boxing stadiums. For these shows in Phuket there were no costs for the sponsored fighters. The gym provided shorts to fight in, made the transport arrangements, paid for all ancillaries needed for the fight and funded the support team.

For shows in Lumpinee, the fight purse for male fighters is THB10,000. Women were not allowed to fight at this stadium at the time of writing. For fighters from outlying areas to fight in the Bangkok stadiums, considerable costs are involved. Flights for the fighter and at least one trainer have to be funded. Sumalee always sent a media person too, so both the fighter and the gym had video record of the fight, which could be used on social media *ad infinitum*. Sumalee funded living costs and hotel accommodation. This involved two nights in a hotel, as the weigh-in for Lumpinee fights is extremely early in the morning. A stay the night after was necessary as well because foreign fighters are last on the programme, often not finishing until around midnight. When Sumalee took fighters to the local stadium in Koh Samui, the situation regarding costs was the same because the fight purse was also low, at around THB8,000. Sumalee recognised the marketing benefits of having fighters fight elsewhere in Thailand, especially if it was at Lumpinee. Consequently, Sumalee made no deductions from the fighter's fight purse and all their expenses were paid.

Among the promotions Sumalee worked with, Thai Fight and Z1 in Malaysia were the most generous with fighter remuneration. The fight purse in these promotions was THB30,000 or more. These promoters also paid for all living and accommodation costs. Sumalee made some deductions from these fight purses to cover expenses accrued by the sponsorship programme.

For tournaments, the stakes were much higher. However, usually the winner 'took all', which meant that other fighters received very little remuneration. Sumalee took a fighter to Omnoi Stadium for a tournament. The winning purse was THB500,000. This was the only time during our period of sponsoring fighters where the financial returns were attractive. The fighter fought two legs, three weeks apart, but was knocked out of the tournament. He earned nothing from the fights. To prepare him leading up to the fights, Sumalee sponsored his nutrition programme, flights, hotels, trainer team, etc. The fighter had the prestige of having fought at Omnoi Stadium, which is a bastion of tradition in the MT world. In reality, the return for Sumalee was minimal. For promotions such as these, the name of the gym the fighter represents is not mentioned in the commentary and the fighter is required to wear the promotion's apparel rather than the gym's. The conclusion must surely be that the fighter gained far more from this opportunity than the sponsoring gym.

The majority of Thai gyms compensate for fight purse shortfalls through earnings derived from gambling and sometimes from sponsorship. For gyms not involved in gambling (and Sumalee is one of them), sponsoring fighters provides no direct financial return. The benefit of sponsoring fighters comes from the ability and expertise of the gym to utilise the achievements of the fighters through online content. This, in turn, promotes the fighter, standing them in good stead for the future.

It is hard for fighters to live on their fight purse unless they receive other support. Those who don't receive any support are financially stressed. They become dissatisfied if the gym makes deductions when the amount of the fight purse warrants it. Many of Sumalee's sponsored fighters had little or no experience with the 'real' world and failed to appreciate the outgoings of running a business. This caused tension between the gym management and the fighters.

Behaviour in the Gym

Although Sumalee is managed in a Western style, the training regime and ethos, especially for fighters, are traditionally Thai. A gym predominantly populated by male fighters, some of whom were extremely narcissistic, needs to have a strict code of conduct in order to survive. The culture in Thailand from the top echelons down, promoted and permeated down through education, is authoritarian. Young minds are trained to be submissive to power, starting with unquestioned obedience to teachers. It filters right down through society. Schools and other institutions are a microcosm of Thailand's totalitarian society. This is the natural order expected within a Thai gym. MT trainers have emerged from a disciplined environment. They do not expect their authority to be questioned, particularly if the person breaking the rules is less experienced and/or younger than them. A minority of our fighters, coming from a different cultural background, found following such a regime challenging. This led to a lot of unpleasantness in the gym at one stage and ultimately to a complete breakdown in the sponsorship programme.

The majority of the fighters were respectful to all the staff. Sadly, this was not the case all the time. There were frictions as well as instances of bullying of staff. Dynamics within a MT gym are complex. If a trainer felt a fighter had stepped out of line, he could be very hard on them. During fight preparation, tension within the gym is high, and controlling what happens in the heat of the moment is a mammoth task. Trainers mimic the regime they were exposed to in the authoritarian gyms they were brought up in. It is not uncommon for MT trainers to be bullies. Sumalee has encountered them and their tenure within the gym is short. Dealing with conflicts within the gym takes a great deal of management skill and time. In a minority of instances, unpleasant behaviour by both sponsored fighters and trainers extended beyond the gym floor. This was unacceptable and dealt with promptly.

Sumalee has a strict policy on how social media is used by fighters. They are specifically prohibited from commenting on other gyms/fighters on social media platforms. Furthermore, they are requested not to get into online arguments on issues relating to the business. Fighters are encouraged to adhere to professional standards of online behaviour at all times. It's regrettable that other gyms do not adhere to similar policies as it would lift standards and potentially attract more people to the sport.

Our customers are the bedrock of our business and how we interact with them is crucial to our survival. Without them, the business is not viable and could not run a sponsored fighter programme. There needs to be clear boundaries between fighters and the customers. Getting involved in personal relationships with the customers, informing and involving them in behind-the-scenes gym issues is frowned upon. The majority of fighters understood and respected these guidelines but there have been exceptions.

Overall, the customers and fighters have enjoyed good relationships and lasting friendships have been formed. Customers enjoy watching them develop as fighters and many follow them on social media after their visit. As mentioned previously, some were hugely generous to the fighters.

At one stage the group of fighters receiving sponsorship became quite large. Some customers reported feeling intimidated or alienated by the group. We even had a case where a sponsored fighter went in heavy on a customer who had upset him for some reason. Obviously this was unacceptable and was dealt with swiftly.

It was common place for some fighters, but certainly not all, to ignore the guidelines on the use of substances which are illegal in Thailand. Only one fighter was ever asked to leave the gym because of drug abuse. There were other reasons for requesting him to leave but his persistent use of drugs classified as illegal in Thailand was involved. Not only did he bring illegal drugs onto the gym premises which contravened the terms of our land lease, he involved the customers too.

Ending the Full Sponsorship Programme

Reflecting over our time of sponsoring foreign fighters, it was a mistake to allow fighters to stay for too long. I believe regular contract reviews as well as refreshing the stable of fighters would have prevented many of the problems we encountered. Unacceptable behaviour was overlooked for too long in the mistaken belief that the fighters were the key to the success of the business.

There were many joyous occasions during the time that we sponsored foreign fighters. Being involved in their careers and watching them progress/win fights were exhilarating. Sadly, there were many disappointments in the way some of them behaved too.

Towards the end of our time of sponsoring foreign fighters, I received a message from a South American fighter. I didn't know the fighter concerned, but he approached us with the right attitude. He was offering something in return for any sponsorship we were able to provide. He promised that he would chart his sponsorship journey and promote the gym with a video he was able to make in co-operation with another of his sponsors. Knowing that he had limited opportunities, I decided we could offer him three months free sponsorship at the gym. He came: staying in an air-conditioned room on-site during a busy time. Normally sponsored fighters stayed outside the gym as paying guests were given priority for the rooms on-site. During his period of sponsorship, he benefitted from some excellent fight opportunities. After the three months, he returned to his home country to work and accrue funds to enable him to return to train in Thailand. When he came back as a paying student, he went to another gym!

Another example of the disappointment we experienced was with a UK fighter who had been training and fighting out of Thailand for several years before any involvement with Sumalee. We knew him and reconnected with him at a Thai Fight event in Koh Samui. Through a member of staff, he asked if we would be prepared to sponsor him because the gym he was training with at the time had some problems. He needed to return to the UK for a fight but asked if he could be sponsored by us in the interim with the promise that after his time in the UK he would return to Sumalee. We took him in, gave him on-site accommodation and arranged a confidence-building fight for him as he had lost a number of fights in sequence. Before he returned to the UK, I gave him some Sumalee branded shorts to wear during his UK fight. This is standard practice for a sponsor. When I watched his UK fight online, I noticed he wasn't wearing the shorts. I asked the staff member who had set the arrangement up why this was. He told me, 'Oh, he's not coming back.' Clearly, he had used our generosity when he had nowhere else to stay, before returning to the UK without any intention of becoming part of our fight team. He didn't even have the courtesy to tell me himself that he was not returning to Thailand.

Perhaps the greatest disappointment and the most reprehensible of all is the way in which some of the fighters we have helped to a very great extent in their careers have used social media to publicly and privately abuse the gym, me personally and my family. There is no excuse whatsoever for this kind of behaviour and only diminishes the image of the sport. It gives no credit to any gym that houses this kind of fighter, often in full knowledge of how much help Sumalee gave to them. More importantly, it ultimately stunts the growth of the sport as it discourages gyms in Thailand from sponsoring foreign fighters.

At the end of 2015/beginning of 2016, we made the decision to stop fully sponsoring foreign fighters, except for a few commitments already in place. Overall, the disadvantages to us of fully sponsoring foreign fighters far outweighed the advantages. (We continue to fully sponsor Thai fighters on a case-by-case basis. We also sponsor Thai gyms where we feel it is appropriate.) Apart from the disappointment, we found that sponsoring foreign fighters led to poor trainer morale and tension in the gym. Trainers put a lot of effort into bringing fighters on only to find the fighter leaving without recourse if it suited them to do so. Trainers were becoming increasingly reluctant to mentor fighters and to give up their free time accompanying them to fights locally and internationally. In the case of one fighter, some of the trainers refused to train him at all because of his attitude.

A number of MT gyms in Phuket have stopped sponsoring foreign fighters for the same reasons as ours. This change in focus by gyms is regrettable and has consequences for the growth and development of foreign fighters.

We were already well underway with plans to reduce our dependence on renowned trainers, fighters and promoters. Changing the focus to wellness was more in tune with our own ethos and aspirations. This period marked a watershed for the business and led to significantly happier and more rewarding times.

I would advise extreme caution to other gym owners when weighing up whether to sponsor foreign fighters. My advice would be to consider only those fighters you know well and who have some means of financial support other than income derived from fighting. Get references from previous gyms they have trained at. Gyms need to cooperate more in order to produce a more satisfactory sponsorship experience. Such co-operation would also encourage fighters to give more consideration to how they conduct themselves during their period of sponsorship.

If a gym owner feels that the fighter is not a positive influence/contributor to the gym, don't hold out in the hope that the gym will produce a superstar who will ultimately make the gym's name. Making real headway as a foreign fighter in Thailand is a difficult task. Whilst a few make their mark and are astute enough to make something of the opportunity they have been given, the majority come and go. More often than not, foreign fighters are used as opponents to boost national pride in the home team. This is the purpose of Thai Fight.

When they leave, don't expect any loyalty from them. In our experience, the opposite is more likely to happen.

The majority of fighters do not have any health protection insurance. We were lucky in that the only fighter who was injured enough to require an operation did have insurance. We lived on a knife edge, hoping that nothing serious ever happened under our watch and we were fortunate that it did not.

There were many happy and rewarding times working with the foreign fighters. Some stayed with us for several years, gaining experience that enabled them to make significant progress in their fight careers. Overall, though, sponsoring foreign fighters is challenging. It is possibly a necessary step in the evolution of a gym but a drain on emotional and financial resources once the gym becomes established.

Chapter 8
Muay Thai Fighter Contracts

I had always thought of human trafficking as the illegal movement of a person from one country to another for the purposes of commercial exploitation, involving restriction of movement and violation of human rights.

But a situation that arose at Sumalee has led me to question whether the contracts imposed on many MT fighters fall under the definition of human trafficking. The fullest definition I found was as follows:

> Human trafficking is the trade of humans for the purpose of forced labour, sexual slavery or commercial exploitation... Human trafficking can occur within a country or trans-nationally. Human trafficking is a crime against the person because of the violation of the victim's rights of movement through coercion and because of their commercial exploitation. Human trafficking is the trade in people and does not necessarily involve the movement of the person from one place to another.   (Source: Wikipedia)

The case of famous fighter Buakaw and his unbreakable gym contract, together with the impact it had on his career, was well publicised, both in Thailand and internationally. Many were shocked at Buakaw's story. From the age of fifteen, Buakaw fought out of Por Pramuk Gym in Bangkok. He remained with the gym for fifteen years. However, in 2012 he fell into dispute with the owners over the cancellation of an exhibition fight in Japan which he was to attend with the then Prime Minister Yingluck Shinawatra. This was the culmination of what he saw as being poor treatment by the gym and in a press conference said, 'I can stand tough training, but not poor treatment. It is about the mind, not the body.' He left the camp and when he subsequently fought on Thai Fight soon afterwards, the owners of Por Pramuk opened a lawsuit against Buakaw and Thai Fight. Thereafter ensued a long legal battle between the boxer and the owners of Por Pramuk. During this period, as he had not been released from this contract with Por Parmuk, he was prevented from fighting Muay Thai.

But how extensive are these restrictive fighter contracts and how should we judge this practice? Not all fighter contracts violate human rights. There are many ethical and responsible fighter managers/gym owners within the MT community. Nevertheless, because the majority of fighters have an association with their gym from a very young age, that freedom of movement for many is severely impeded.

I am not able to name the gym involved in this story, as the defamation laws in Thailand are extremely strict.

> Under Section 326 of the Thai Criminal Code, defamation is defined as whoever imputes anything about another person to a third person in a manner likely to impair the person's reputation or place the person in contempt or hatred of others. To do so can lead to imprisonment.

I wish only to raise awareness, not to defame.

Sumalee needed to recruit a trainer. We were introduced to a young fighter from Nakhon Si Thammarat by one of our trainers who was also from that area. The fighter (to protect his identity and that of his gym he will hereafter be referred to as Nak) was 19 years old at the time. It was explained to us that he was a promising up-and-coming fighter but had problems with his previous gym. Consequently he left the gym he was under contract to.

When Nak joined us, he made several complaints about how he had been treated at the gym he had grown up in. He claimed his treatment was such that he was unable to train effectively or focus. It is not appropriate for me to go into the detail of these complaints, as I have not heard the other side of the story. Suffice to say Nak became so unhappy at the gym that he left without any notice, just prior to a fight where the gym stood to earn a good purse and no doubt significant earnings from gambling too. The gym owners (there were two of them) were furious with him. As far as we were concerned, this was nothing to do with us and his fight contract did not prohibit him from working as a trainer for us. So, we employed him. He was a very good trainer, popular with the fighters and customers alike.

As Nak was such a promising young fighter and was now based in Phuket, he was much in demand with the local fight promoters. The promise of a great new matchup plus the potential gambling profits will always get them excited. So, Nak took part in two fights in Phuket's stadiums. Everyone involved in setting up this fight were aware of his situation including the stadium owners and the local promoters.

In the Bangkok stadiums where the most prestigious and important fight promotions take place, in order to fight, fighters must show their Sports Authority 'blue registration book'. The gym usually holds onto this, as was the case with Nak. This is normal practice. It is also not unusual for fighters who have left the gym they have a contractual agreement with, for whatever reason, to go fight in provinces where it is not necessary to show the Sports Authority blue registration book. This usually happens without any repercussions. The fight purse in these provinces is minimal (around THB6,000) and the fighters cannot progress their careers via this route so the managing gym owner is typically untroubled by it.

This was not the case with Nak's gym. They were furious. They staged a two-pronged attack; one against Nak and his family, and the other against Sumalee. We received very real threats from a lawyer acting on their behalf, requiring a payment of THB2,000,000 (USD65,000) to compensate them for loss of earning, which if not paid within a certain time period would result in court action.

What was even more alarming was that our lawyer informed us the gym owner had a case because we had made him 'lose face', even though our gym received no payment at all for the fight. Interestingly, in contrast to the Buakaw case, no blame at all was attached to the Thai promoters who set the fight up, despite their being more aware of the likely consequences than we were.

As we dug deeper into Nak's story we became deeply concerned about his predicament and what was probably the situation of many other fighters. Not only was his contract (which we had a copy of) one-sided, there appeared to be no official body that could represent the rights of fighters such as him. If there was, we didn't find it, and we tried extremely hard. The contract laid out all the conditions Nak was required to meet but none of the conditions the gym had to meet. The contract did specify the fight frequency he could expect, which apparently was not adhered to.

Nak's story was not uncommon in the MT world. His father was an unworldly man from Southern Thailand, who became a trainer at the gym in Bangkok. He took Nak with him and from a young age Nak was housed, fed, trained and schooled by the gym. I understand his father was not paid a wage but worked for his keep and that of his son. It soon became apparent Nak was a very talented and strong fighter; and thereby a valuable commercial asset to the gym.

At 18 Nak was offered a ten-year contract with the gym. Bear in mind, at this stage, he had never known anything else. His life had been at the gym and his family felt beholden to them as the gym had taken care of them. It was more than likely they didn't appreciate that there had been an exchange with the work the father had done for the gym. They would have seen the gym owners as benefactors and would have been unaware of any other options available to them. Nak's father handed ownership of his son's career over to the gym by signing a contract even though he was unlikely to have understood the terminology used in the contract given his educational level.

When the gym in Bangkok found out Nak had fought in Phuket, their first strategy was to contact his parents and request a payment of THB200,000 from them. The letter stipulated that if the parents could not pay then Nak was to return to the gym immediately, even if it was against his will. His parents, who are extremely poor, were petrified and Nak was desperately worried. However, for whatever reason, he still refused to go back to the gym despite all the threats. To return would have been very much against his will.

Following this, we encouraged Nak to go to the gym and request to be released from the contract for a payment from us of THB200,000. This was the amount the gym had requested from his parents so we felt it was a fair offer.

We accompanied Nak to the gym and honestly, I was shocked at the extent to which he literally prostrated himself in apology to the gym owners. This demonstrated to me how much power he felt that gym owners had over him. To save his face, the gym owner took photographs of Nak prostrating himself, which were then published in *Muay Siam*, a popular MT magazine. I now know this behaviour is expected and common place as illustrated in a *Bangkok Post* report of Buakaw's meeting with his gym owner under similar circumstances.

During our meeting with the gym owners, the photographer also attempted to take photos of us without our permission, presumably for them to be published too. I told them this was not acceptable. Nevertheless, we later found that our photos had been published. I understand that the data protection law came into effect in Thailand this year (2021), which hopefully should protect people from such invasions of privacy.

The meeting was intimidating and humourless. No one introduced themselves (which is common in Thailand), so we had no idea who we were talking to. It did become apparent, however, that there was someone giving them legal advice at the meeting. They made it clear that Nak was not for sale and that if he didn't return to their gym he would never fight again. It was their view that he owed them everything because he had been brought up in their gym. No acknowledgement of the contribution he had made to the reputation and earnings of the gym was ever made. As far as they were concerned, he belonged to them and was very much in their debt. Nothing was resolved at this meeting. The meeting ended in a stalemate.

It was after this meeting that the threats to Sumalee started coming. We received a letter from a lawyer's office laying out their case and the demand for payment of THB2,000,000.

This they claimed was compensation in lieu of loss of earnings from Nak over the remaining years in his contract.

Nak's plight was as worrying to me as the threats from the gym. We looked in every direction we knew to try and find an appropriate course to deal with this matter. Our objective was to find a mutually acceptable way for him to continue with his promising career. We spoke to anyone we knew who might have some insight into how we could solve the problem. We contacted Thai gym owners we knew, prominent foreigners involved in MT in Thailand, lawyers, the World Muaythai Council and the Sports Authority in both Phuket and Bangkok.

Finally, the Sports Authority in Bangkok agreed to arbitrate between Nak and the gym owners. This literally meant chairing a meeting and nothing more. We paid for a lawyer to accompany Nak to this meeting. She attempted to negotiate on his behalf, however her conclusion was that they only had one objective, which was to seek revenge and take Sumalee to court. Nak was absolutely not for sale. She subsequently declined to get involved further as she found the gym owners unpleasant and intimidating. Stories about Muay Thai Mafia may well have been in the back of her mind. The events concern the activities Klaew Thanikul, a Thai-Chinese entrepreneur and gym owner, in the 1980s and 90s. Although these gangland style activities took place many years ago, the repercussions on the reputation of Muay Thai reverberate for generations.

Fortunately, we did receive good legal advice ourselves at this time. Regarding the summons made to us, our lawyer advised us not to respond at all. She explained that there was a two-year time-scale between the event in question (Nak's fight) and the gym owners being able to take action against us. We were already eighteen months into that.

After not responding to their summons, a subsequent

meeting was set up by the Sports Authority in Bangkok acting as an arbitrator. Rhian acted as the translator during this meeting. The gym's owners had become slightly more conciliatory, but nevertheless were attended by a lawyer, and agreed to sell Nak for THB500,000. This is a high price for a fighter who had not yet made his name. At my previous gym, my business partner and I had jointly purchased Saenchai for THB600,000, and Saenchai is one of the most famous and accomplished MT fighters in the world. This gives an idea of how inflated the asking price for Nak was. The Sports Authority did encourage them to consider a lower offer and they came back with THB400,000. This was still a grossly inflated figure and consequently negotiations broke down.

These events occurred in 2016–2017. Nak has never been released from his contract. After the hullabaloo, he decided to go to work in China to release the grip that the gym had on him here in Thailand. He has never fought since. His contract will expire in a couple of years, by which time he will be 28 years old and well past his fighting prime.

How should we as MT tourists react to stories such as these? No matter how integrated we think we are into the MT community in Thailand, most of us are only passing through. We stay for a while and then we go back to our lives in the West, often not having any further involvement in the world of MT. Do we have any right to question such contracts? What can be done? Something that never fails to astonish me is that despite knowing that a gym has a poor record with regard to how they treat their staff and/or their fighters, people who should know better still support these gyms. In Thailand, they are prepared the overlook standards that would horrify people in their home countries.

We all understand that life is very different here in Thailand and that MT does serve a positive purpose, especially for poor families. However, Westerners boycott companies who have a poor human rights record and who take advantage of their workforce. For some reason, the MT community seems unprepared to look deeper into how gyms conduct their business.

I would like to see a time when MT tourists start to look under the surface of the gyms they are patronising. Questions that should be asked are: How are the fighters recruited? What rights do they have? Who is taking care of their welfare, and how? What about the staff? What contracts are they on? What rights do they have under Thai labour laws (yes, there are Thai labour laws and they are similar to those of the UK).

During the time of the Covid-19 crisis, these issues were more transparent that they'd ever been. What happened to all the fighters and the trainers at the gyms? Where did they all go? Who took care of them? Was the training staff eligible for social security payments as they should have been? To the best of my knowledge, the vast majority had to go back to their homes and rely on their families. One well-known gym even put their fighters up for sale. It later transpired that this step was taken without the fighters' knowledge or permission. As the pandemic dragged on, other gyms also tried to sell their fighters although in these cases I am unsure whether the fighters were in agreement or not. Some might argue that more informal mechanisms of support were in place, where dependents were reliant on the generosity and goodwill of the gym owner. Such a system is not without merit, but it places the receiver even further in the debt of the gym owner. This is the system that appears to be pervasive and all too frequently results in an abuse of power by those in charge.

Others might counter that this is the Thai way of doing things and we shouldn't interfere. But should we condone and support such practices? Many of us have experienced disappointment when we've invested in someone only to find that they leave our business for another one. No matter how much we've invested in a person, does that give us the right to block their career for ten years? Shouldn't a fighter contract be like an employment contract where we invest in the hope of receiving a return but where the person contracted also has rights? Shouldn't there be a body that looks after the fighter's interests and is there to represent them if needed? A body that is accessible. Who can a fighter turn to in the event of such problems? Most would not have enough money to employ a lawyer and their families would not be able to help them either financially or have enough experience to provide the right guidance. If an official body does exist to represent the interests of fighters in Thailand, I certainly don't know of it and neither do the many people I contacted regarding this issue.

If nothing else, it is my hope that this story will encourage people to look more deeply into what they are buying/involving themselves in and do the right thing, which in the long run will only benefit the MT community, especially the fighters who are at the bottom of the ladder.

This experience, amongst others, certainly led me to question the extent I wanted our business to be involved in the fight community, the majority of which is run archaically and is unregulated. The fight side of the business is exciting but to be involved in it to any degree comes at great moral cost. It was one of a few pivots that led us to look at our business and reconsider the direction we were going in.

As an addendum to this story, there has been a development that some may regard as perplexing. The trainer/fighter in question here had to return from China to Thailand having lost his job at the start of the pandemic. I noticed some posts by him on his social media referring to the owner of the gym he was contracted to as 'his father' in an affectionate way. Sadly, I have a suspicion that there is motive behind such public terms of endearment. Now that the fighter/trainer will need to pursue his career in Thailand, whatever direction that might take, he will be aware that the gym owner of his youth may well have a lot of influence over what happens to him next.

Chapter 9
Muay Thai Promotions

Writing generically about fight promotions in Thailand is a mammoth task because the volume and variety of fight promotions have increased exponentially in recent years. The level of interest generated by the Ultimate Fighting Championship (UFC) promotion may have been a stimulus for this, demonstrating as it did that there is a keen audience for combat sports.

The shows in Thailand are not only geographically spread out, but also managed and funded in very different ways. Sumalee has sent fighters all over Thailand and other parts of Asia, as well as to Europe, the USA and Central America. However, expert knowledge of this disparate field only comes from close involvement in it over a long period. Nevertheless, by sharing some of my experiences, I hope to help you understand more about fight promotions in Thailand. As one of the few (if only) foreign women who have had any experience in promoting fights in Thailand, the anecdotes shared here give a unique perspective.

Since 2010 Sumalee fighters have appeared on most of the top shows in Thailand featuring foreigners on the fight card, including Thai Fight; Top King World Series; Max Muay Thai; Toyota Cup; MX Muay Thai Extreme; Super Muay Thai; King's Cup; Queen's Birthday; Kunlun Fight; Legend of Victor; and promotions at the Bangkok stadiums of Lumpinee and Omnoi etc. Over this period we have seen many promotions come and go. Thai Fight, funded by the public purse, is beginning to look like the 'old man' of fight promotions here. One might legitimately ask many questions as to why so many promotions fail. What's behind it? Does it impact on the future or credibility of the sport? What's the solution?

One Championship (established in 2011) is leading the field in a new era of fight promotions for Asia with a different philosophy. Unlike their predecessors in the fight promotions business, their long-term strategy aligns with the business model of social media giant Facebook. Their short-term goal is to build audiences, using their athletes as influencers, and once achieved they will go to the broadcasters and advertisers to seek lucrative broadcasting deals. Although the promotion has yet to make a profit, fighters are optimistic that it heralds more opportunities and better pay cheques for them.

(Coincidentally at the time of writing this chapter, it has been announced that the social media personality Gary Vaynerchuk has become involved in the MMA business in the USA. In this interview Gary expresses his belief that, using his online marketing expertise and involvement, MMA will become one of the three greatest sports in the world, alongside basketball and football (soccer). It will be interesting to watch how his approach will impact the combat sports business in general in the long term.)

A Male Domain

Given my unique role here in Thailand, it would be an omission if I didn't write about some of my experiences as a woman in the context for fight promotions. The lowly role of women in MT is a subject of much discussion, particularly amongst female foreign fighters.

Thai women in general are much more accepting of their lowly role in MT, and in society. That's how life is here and they don't expect anything different. Thai society is much more misogynistic than appears on the surface. To a large extent, sadly, women are complicit in this because they see themselves as having much lower economic value than men and are therefore subservient to them.

Sanitsuda Ekachai, a columnist in the *Bangkok Post*, writes extensively about misogyny in Thai society. Emma Thomas, a British teacher and fighter living in Thailand for many years, also writes extensively on the subject, often in the context of MT.

I am frequently asked whether being woman is an obstacle when it comes to doing business in Thailand. My answer to this is that there are many other obstacles to overcome which are much greater. When it comes to MT shows and promotions, however, my own experience is that being female is not without its drawbacks.

The world of MT is historically very much a male domain. The MT ring is regarded as sacrosanct. Women who menstruate are not! In the opinion of many, therefore, a woman should never go across the ring. This is why they are not allowed to enter the ring over the ropes; they must go under.

For someone like myself, this is much more difficult than it appears. I have been required to enter the ring at shows on many occasions to be photographed with a fighter or to present a belt to a winner. Often there are thousands of people watching. In the early days, I usually ended up crawling through the ropes in an inelegant way. After studying more agile and much younger female fighters making a much better job of their entry into the ring, I came to realise there is a technique which if followed obviates the need to crawl in. It involves dropping to the knees just outside the ropes, bending one's torso beneath the ropes and somehow managing to get up off your knees with some semblance of dignity. I am getting there!

In many of the oldest, most prestigious stadiums, women are not allowed to touch the ring, let alone enter it (although it is noted that this is likely to change with an announcement in May 2021 that women will be allowed to fight at Lumpinee). I remember being shocked when taking ringside photos at a traditional gym in Bangkok and being admonished for stepping over the gloves and paraphernalia sitting on the perimeter of the ring. This is frowned upon as it leads to the possibility that a (dirty) menstruating woman may open her legs across the gloves etc.

One particularly upsetting experience of how women are often treated at stadiums was when I had taken fighters to a promotion in Koh Samui. I had driven a minivan all the way from Phuket, with an early start to get to the stadium for the weigh-in on the day of the show. The weigh-in completed, the fighters were relaxing whilst I was sitting in the stadium listening to music, not bothering anyone. A security guard approached and ordered me in an impolite way to wait outside until the show opened. I explained that I was a gym owner and I had driven a long way to bring fighters to the show to help the promoter. I emphasised that I was tired and not prepared to wait standing outside in the heat. He was about to physically eject me when the promoter saw what was happening and came to my rescue. I know with complete certainty that if I had been a Thai man, let alone a gym owner, I would not have been treated in this way.

There is one promoter at Bangla Boxing Stadium in Phuket who, over the course of ten years of my taking fighters there, has never once acknowledged me. Given that gyms train and provide the fighters who are the lifeblood of a promoter's livelihood, this hardly seems the most appropriate and sensible business approach. There is an owner of a small stadium in Chalong who is so openly rude and hostile to women that I refuse to send any fighter there at all.

Fortunately, this is not the case with all promoters and from some I have received the utmost respect. One promoter at Bangla Boxing Stadium did me the honour of including me on a poster celebrating the contribution of the main gyms within Phuket to his promotions.

On a positive note, if you are a Thai woman and ergo perceived as having low earning power, where there is an admission fee, you will pay less than the men! This practice reflects the longstanding and widely held view that women are able to contribute little to the economic vitality of the country.

An 'Incidental' Promoter

My early days as an 'incidental' promoter were a baptism of fire. Looking back now I realise just how naive I was when I signed up to MT gym ownership in Thailand, particularly with regard to the fight side of the business. I knew nothing about it. My business partner was responsible for this aspect of the business. I played a more strategic role and relied on whoever was more appropriately qualified to deal with promoters, arranging fights etc. At Sumalee, the head or senior trainer is given this responsibility.

Whilst I have many qualms about how the fight side of the business is run in Thailand, involvement in it is infectious and exciting. I have travelled in motorcades, and armed guards have surrounded me. Where else do you get such experiences?

Taking fighters to top-ranked promotions is exhilarating, filling you with expectation and hope. Over time, however, you realise you are being beguiled. More often than not, the odds are stacked heavily against foreign fighters in one way or another. Lack of standardisation in scoring techniques is one reason for this. There are many other reasons too.

MT fighter, and subsequently entertainer, Samart Payakaroon discusses the lack of standardisation in scoring here, although I don't agree with his conclusion. Being scored on parameters other than striking is a large part of the appeal of MT and its distinctive beauty as a combat sport. I believe that to preserve it, the heritage of the sport must not be diluted.

In Thailand, most promoters are revered and perceived as having great power and wealth. For Thai fighters/gym owners, to be a promoter is regarded as the Holy Grail, the pinnacle of achievement within the MT community. For foreign fighters, they are the gateway to bigger opportunities in the future.

If you are a fighter, especially a fledgling one, you would be wise not to upset a promoter. Promoters are influential and they have a long reach within the MT community. Local promoters in tourist hubs like Phuket are the pathway to much bigger opportunities elsewhere. One young fighter we sponsored upset a local promoter by declining an opportunity to fight on a New Year special show because he didn't want to train over Christmas. The fighter was offered no further interesting fight opportunities.

In another case, a fighter who was new to us upset a well-known promoter in Bangkok by writing an unfavourable review of his gym (this particular fighter is now well known for this type of behaviour). The promoter was angry and informed the fighter that if he didn't take the review offline, he would never get another fight in Thailand.

My own role as a promoter was entirely incidental. My

co-owner in the gym I invested in craved to be a promoter, as he knew this would give him considerable standing within the MT community. My investment in the gym gave him the opportunity to dip his toe in the water of MT show promotion.

Whilst I had returned to the UK to work on a research project, without any consultation with me, the gym's co-owner masterminded a show in Patthalung in the south of Thailand. He was from the area and being a promoter in a show so near to his home would have given him a considerable amount of prestige locally. It was an all Thai fighter show and we took one fighter from our gym, who at the time was the Southern Thailand Champion. I returned in time to attend the event but was not involved in any of the details of this show except to be told at the end that we made a profit of THB50,000. This had barely covered the costs of getting the team down to Patthalung and the associated accommodation/living costs.

I am not sure what weight cut was required but I know it was harsh. The weigh-in was on the morning of the fight. This was my first experience behind the scenes of a weigh-in. The fighter was so weak, he could barely stand. It was only much later that I became aware of how dangerous weight cutting can be. Fortunately, the fighter's weight was on point, as I don't believe he would have had the strength to lose any more weight.

Once the weigh-in was complete, the fighter was taken to the place where he was staying to rest while an intravenous drip was administered by the trainers. Such practice is common. Often fighters will attend a clinic following a weigh-in to have an intravenous drip administered. At least when it is done at a clinic, there is some semblance of safety involved.

Unfortunately, the fighter was unable to recover from his very weakened state. He lost the fight and the gym's side bet of THB50,000 (nullifying any profit made on the promotion).

I noted when we returned to the gym in Phuket, many of the trainers would not speak to the fighter for several days because he had lost the fight and presumably their contribution to the side bet. MT is a hard sport in more ways than one!

High Stakes

I have attended many promotions in rural and outlying areas, both in Thailand and Malaysia. They are always well attended, as there is little else in outdoor entertainment offered. What is most striking is the heavy preponderance of males within the audience.

It will come as no surprise to anyone who knows anything about the MT scene in Thailand that there is always a high proportion of gamblers at these shows. Tensions are often high and the show in Patthalung was no exception. Things can turn ugly rather quickly. The referee team at the show were from Phuket. There was a fighter from the well-known gym in Phuket, Singpatong Sitnumnoi gym (SSG). This fighter was the underdog so the odds were against him winning. However, the SSG fighter was judged by the referees to have won. There was a point in the immediate aftermath where I feared for my life! The crowd went ballistic and I was very pleased to be at the front with an under-the-ring escape plan in mind. Fights broke out. Things were thrown into the ring including chairs, bottles and anything else the disgruntled punters could lay their hands on. Nobody wanted to take control of the situation, least of all my co-promoter. This gave a great deal of insight into his character, as he was ultimately responsible for the promotion.

It was Num Noi, the owner of SSG, who was brave enough to get into the ring and calm the situation down. My Thai wasn't strong at the time so I am unsure as to what he said, but it seemed to do the trick. This was not the only time I witnessed such a commotion triggered by the gamblers attending a local show.

At a show I attended in Nakhon Si Thammarat, a fight broke out among the gamblers there. This area of Thailand has a reputation for mafia-like activities. The Thai I was with told me it was not beyond the realms of possibility that such a skirmish would lead to someone being shot later. It is of no surprise that so few women choose to attend. It is not unheard of for people to lose their lives over disputes related to gambling.

In another video by Samart Payakaroon, the detrimental effects of gambling on the sports and its image are highlighted.

Throwing things into a MT ring is seen as disrespectful as the ring is regarded as sacrosanct. I remember watching a show at Bangla Boxing Stadium in Phuket when a drunken Australian punter, dissatisfied with the referee's decision over a fight, threw a chair into the ring. Within milliseconds the referee in the ring had jumped over the ropes (in a manner he looked incapable of) and together with the other referees and security guards very aggressively evicted the culprit out of the stadium.

International Team Match-ups

The second real eye-opener for me happened early on in my involvement in the Muay Thai business. A team of six fighters was taken to South Korea to fight in the 2010 WAKO PRO World Challenge. Although our business had nothing to do with the promotion of the show, our gym was responsible for the recruitment of most of the non-Korean fighters. This was my first real experience of absolute misogyny within the Asian fight world. I was completely ignored by the Korean males involved in the organisation of the show. I was perplexed as I had never experienced this is in my business life before.

The fights were arranged over two days. The first day was disastrous with losses by all the fighters we had taken over. They were outclassed by the more experienced K1 opponents. I was concerned about the poor match-ups and how this reflected on the image of our gym's competency. It was explained to me that we had taken a team of fighters over to Korea to lose, as a debt of favour was owed to the promoter of the show. The objective of the show was to make the local national team look good. Sacrificing one's own business reputation in this way was completely new to me.

One of the fighters we took with us to Korea was Valdet Gashi, who later achieved ignominy through joining ISIS in Syria and was subsequently killed in unknown circumstances in 2015. Valdet was an Albanian who grew up in Germany from the age of 6. He came to Thailand to pursue a professional fighting career in 2009. At the WAKO show he was matched against Lim Chi Bin, the South Korean welterweight champion. This fight illustrates the concern I had about the match-ups which were in the main very uneven, with the visiting team being at a disadvantage.

Valdet was injured in the fight, and suffered serious injuries to the face. Like the majority of fighters in Thailand, who mostly live a hand-to-mouth existence, Valdet had limited resources to pay for hospital treatment. However, he knew his rights and he stood his ground in a very impressive way, which was admirable for someone so young. He insisted that the promoter arrange for him to go to hospital on the evening of the fight. The hospital wouldn't treat him immediately. They said it was necessary for the internal bleeding to stop first.

The promoter wanted him to leave the country with the rest of the team the next day, with the promise he would attend to his medical bills in Thailand. Valdet didn't trust him and absolutely refused to leave until the necessary operation had been undertaken and paid for. When the promoter tried to insist that he leave, Valdet threatened to go to the police as all the foreign fighters had entered the country without the appropriate visas. This got the promoter's attention as he realised Valdet meant business. I couldn't help but admire Valdet for his determination.

Valdet's story is a lesson to all fighters in shows outside their home country. It is wise either to have the right insurance covering you or, better still, to make sure the promoter is in a position to look after you should you sustain a serious injury in a fight.

One of our fighters sustained a similar injury when he fought in a charity show arranged to raise funds for Superlek Sorn Esaan's wife following his premature death in his early forties (see Chapter 10). The fight was in Ubon Ratchathani and the promoter concerned took no care whatsoever of the injured fighter. Our fighter was fortunate in that he was insured.

I am unsure what the regulations stipulate about having a qualified medical attendant at fight shows in Thailand. In the bigger shows such as Thai Fight, Toyota Cup and Top King, there was a medical check-up the day before the fight. At regularly held local shows, for example at Bangla Boxing Stadium or Patong Boxing Stadium, there is a health worker (equivalent of a nurse) in attendance. In rural local shows, there is little evidence of qualified medical back-up that I know of.

Thai Fight and Z1

Promotions differ widely with respect to the levels of support offered to fighters and the budgets available to pay the fighters. In terms of the overall packages offered, two of the best promotions we have taken fighters to are Thai Fight and Z1 International. Both of these shows pay the fighters a respectable fight purse, take care of accommodations, contribute to travel expenses and provide sustenance for the fighters.

Over the twelve years that I have been in Thailand, I have attended many Thai Fight shows. Sumalee fighters have fought in the shows throughout Thailand and in Vietnam too. Our fighters have fought Iquezangkor, Provit Aor Piroyapinyo, Kong Samui, Saenchai, Payak Samui, Victor Pinto and Petchrungrueng.

Thai Fight remains my favourite promotion to attend. The standard is high, even though the show is primarily designed to engender feelings of national pride and superiority. The production is of a high calibre and reminiscent of a rock concert. In the first Thai Fight quarter-finals they even had Sek Loso, a famous Thai rock star, entertaining the crowd during an interval. The Thai Fight promotion is designed to provide the highest level of entertainment. To achieve this, fighters are encouraged to be fast and pacey. Clinching, which is highly technical and slows the pace, is discouraged. Since fighters have a natural tendency to fall into the clinch, the referee is kept very busy throughout the bout to ensure the clinch is broken quickly. Fighters are offered a bonus for a KO.

I have many positive things to say about the Thai Fight promotion, not least of which is that it was the forerunner in raising the bar for the standard of promotions in Thailand. It demonstrated that a MT show had the potential to attract huge live audiences in the country across a wide social spectrum, albeit a show which is free to enter because it is sponsored. Thai Fight has the benefit that it does not need to make a profit because it is sponsored by national and local governments. Despite all the positive things I have to say about the show, it has not gone without my notice that the lead people in the promotion treat me, a woman and a gym owner, very differently from my male counterparts.

One of the most memorable Thai Fight shows I attended was in Narathiwat, one of Thailand's most southerly provinces. This province is one of the three involved in the South Thailand Insurgency, an ethnic and religious separatist insurgency. It started in 1948 and has become increasingly violent. The following is an excerpt from a blog post I wrote about the experience.

> When Thai Fight contacted Sumalee Boxing Gym and asked us to take a fighter to their show in Narathiwat in the Thai Southern Provinces, we saw it as a good opportunity to showcase our fighter. We had all heard of the troubles in the Thai Southern Provinces and of our own Foreign Office's advice not to go there unless the journey was necessary. In consequence, we accepted the fight with a certain amount of trepidation.
>
> Provinces in Thailand pay to have the Thai Fight promotion held in their area for a number of reasons. Senior government officials in Narithiwat Province had requested that Thai Fight be staged there in order to instil confidence in the region as a safe destination to visit. Although quite a few people suggested that I should not go, my feeling was that if I

was prepared to send my staff and my fighter, I should be prepared to go there myself.

Concerns over the trip escalated somewhat when a bomb that killed and injured many people was detonated at the Erawan Shrine in Bangkok, a few days before the planned trip. As no one had claimed responsibility for this act there was speculation that this might be related to the insurgency in the south of Thailand.

It was a long drive from Phuket to Narathiwat and despite setting off reasonably early in the morning we arrived in the region after dark. The extent of the trouble in the area was immediately apparent by the numerous military checkpoints, patrols and barricades. It was all very reminiscent of Belfast during the height of the problems in the 1960s and 70s. The fact that development between the towns in this area is sparse meant that it was extremely dark with little or no road lighting. It was easy to be unprepared for the many barricades and checkpoints along the route. Nerves were on edge. Nevertheless, we arrived at the Imperial Hotel in Narathiwat safely. We were pleasantly surprised by the standard of hotel, given that the town is likely to attract little or no tourism and business activity was apparently minimal.

Concerns about terrorism in the locality meant that most of the members of the Thai Fight entourage were reluctant to leave the hotel. There appeared to be little to do in the area anyway as the region is undeveloped for tourism and there is a heavy Muslim influence.

As a result, a feeling of camaraderie was fostered inside the hotel, similar to that found in a siege situation. On the day of the fight, the Thai Fight entourage had a military escort to the stadium. The feeling of danger was heightened by the number of police and military at the hotel from first thing in the morning. A bomb disposal squad was also present. Additionally, five small incendiary devices had been found in the vicinity of the stadium the night before. This had been reported on the news and all the Thais were aware of the situation.

When we arrived at the stadium the security again was heavy. The military and the police were now being backed up by Special Forces (who incidentally were wearing T-shirts very similar to the Thai Fight ones with the name of their organisation emblazoned on the collar, designed to be worn up). Helicopters patrolled constantly and there were more machine guns in evidence than I have ever seen before. Watching what was going on and understanding some of what was being relayed through walkie-talkies, it was clear that the potential for some kind of terrorist attack was real.

When they opened the gates at least two hours before the show started, the people of the province literally came flooding in. By the time the show started there were tens of thousands of spectators. I had plenty of time to kill before the fights started and was able to people-watch for several hours. There was an overriding sense of expectation and joy amongst the crowd, who were predominantly and clearly very poor. I cannot even begin to put an estimate on how many photos were taken before, during and after the show. So many mobile phones (mostly old and outdated models) were in operation that the local cell towers became overloaded and shut down for a while.

The Thai Fight show was more than likely the biggest event to have taken place in the province for a very long time and the people responded wholeheartedly. They came out in hoards, even though at the start of the event there was a heavy downpour with the most impressive lightning I have ever seen anywhere in Thailand (or indeed the world!). The crowd was buzzing throughout the whole of the evening. The fighters were their superstars for the night and they couldn't get enough of them. This was clearly evidenced at the end of the evening when it was impossible to leave the stadium for several hours. Eventually all of the fighters had to leave the stadium under heavy escort in order to make their way through.

At the end of it all, despite a considerable amount of consternation about staging the event in the Southern Provinces, I couldn't help but feel that as far as the local people were concerned the decision was inspired. It was a great gift to the local people. This Thai Fight was about a lot more than winning or losing. It was about giving something to a people who live day to day under the threat of terrorism. The event gave them something to look forward to and a memory to cherish for a long time. I am sure it must have given them hope that there can be a normality.

The Z1 Malaysian promotion fell by the wayside due a failure to judge the extent of interest in MT in the wider Malaysian market. We took fighters to shows in Kelantan and Langkawi (prior to an ill-fated show held in Kuala Lumpur). These Malaysian states all border Thailand and the shows were well attended, although I have no idea whether they were profitable or not.

Encouraged by the apparent level of interest, Z1 decided to host a much bigger show in Kuala Lumpur with Saenchai headlining the show. Despite spending a considerable amount of money and effort on promoting the show, the level of interest was overestimated. The promoters accrued a huge loss and have since ceased promoting.

This Z1 show was held in Stadium Negara, Kuala Lumpur. I do not have any inside information on the cost of hiring this stadium. However, I do know that in many cases stadium owners are the only ones to be assured of a fixed return on a promotion. There is no risk at all involved for the stadium owners.

My experience in the outlying Malaysian states was similar to that in Korea, where as a woman I was ignored. On arrival in Kedah, a Malaysian state bordering Thailand, we were met at the border by the promoters (who were not Z1 on this occasion). A motorcade took us to our hotel. This was exciting and a first for me. When we reached the hotel, there was a welcoming party of local male officials. They shook hands with all the fighters and trainers in our group but ignored me. Earlier holidays in Penang, an island which attracts many overseas visitors, had not alerted me to how fundamentally Muslim much of the rest of the country is.

Local Stadiums

At the gym I invested in, we put on many shows at Bangla Boxing Stadium. This was ten years ago so the figures may be out of date. Generally speaking, however, prices have not changed a great deal since that time. This is a breakdown of the costs involved in putting on a show at Bangla Boxing Stadium in Phuket in 2010/2011, (all prices in THB):

- Cost of hiring the stadium Sunday night, 80,000, and other nights of the week, 120,000
- Cost of posters, 3,000
- Bribe to police to allow posters to go up, 3,000
- Referee team, 12,000
- Payment to attendant health worker, 1,000
- Payment to door staff (two people), 1,000
- Payment to security staff, 2,000
- Payment to ring announcer, 1,000
- Payment to ringside commentator, 1,000
- Payment to ancillary staff (corner cleaners, gate openers, fighter liaison), 3,000
- Payment to fighters (assume eight matchups), 60,000

In 2010, the period when I was incidentally involved in promotions, the promoter received THB800 per ticket. (This was subsequently increased to THB1,000 per ticket, but I don't know if outgoings went up at the same time.) Thais do not pay entrance fees at either Bangla or Patong Boxing Stadiums. This means that to break even on a show at Bangla, at least two hundred tickets must be sold to foreigners for a Sunday show and 250 on other days of the week. The shows I was involved with ran from November to March, Phuket's high season. Only on one show did we sell an excess of two hundred tickets. This was the show with Saenchai and Saiyok on the fight card. The profit on this promotion was THB300,000. This helped to even out the losses made on all the other shows. And this was in high season!

With the growth in opportunities to fight elsewhere, criticism of shows in tourist hubs has increased with some fighters regarding these venues as not worthy of them. There are of course, and always have been, concerns relating to mismatches and failure to conduct weigh-ins. I have on many occasions witnessed fights which were nothing short of dangerous. Nevertheless, fighting in these arenas gives novice fighters a chance to showcase and fine-tune their skills. If they have talent, it will lead to opportunities to fight in more prestigious shows. Shows in tourist hubs should be viewed as a rite of passage for fighters coming to train in Thailand. Being moved up to the next level requires a considerable amount of skill. Talented fighters who have charisma too will not be short of opportunities once they are discovered.

In Phuket, there are usually shows either at Bangla or Patong Boxing Stadium six days a week. The sheer volume of shows is a significant contributor to low attendance figures on a nightly basis. Some would say the calibre of the shows has deteriorated in recent years too. Changes in immigration laws have made it more difficult for fighters to train in Thailand on a long-term basis. Also, fewer gyms are sponsoring fighters. Some of the reasons for this are discussed in Chapter 7 on sponsored fighters.

Fighters aside, the overall growth in demand for MT training has required gyms to grow as businesses too. Gyms in tourist hubs must now be registered as businesses rather than simply being registered with the Sports Authority. With this change, there has been a corresponding uptick in overheads. Gym owners have realised that relying on a stable of sponsored fighters is not a viable way of meeting these increased costs unless the gym is heavily involved in gambling or has a sponsor with deep pockets. The majority of promotions are simply not profitable enough to pay fighters a fight purse, which is adequate to support the fighter and the overheads of a gym.

For gyms, therefore, fighters potentially become overheads rather than assets. For the fighters, it's difficult too as the majority are not able to earn enough. Unless they have the support of their families, or sponsors, staying in Thailand on a long-term basis is not sustainable. In a public post on Facebook, one fighter commented:

> Never let anyone tell you muay thai fighting and staying in Thailand is a glamorous lifestyle! Biggest fight of my life next week. Reduced purses due to Covid, have to pay my own flights and hotel for my coach and I out of it.
>
> After everything paid out, I'll have hardly any left for going toe to toe with one of the best Thai fighters ever!! If I get cut, I'll also need to pay medical bill from that as well.
>
> Erin Kowal, July 2020

With little return for the promoters, the gym owners and even the fighters, MT promotions are in the doldrums. Covid-19 has exacerbated the problems and put a halt to all proceedings. The pandemic has resulted in many foreign fighters leaving Thailand either because their visa did not allow them to stay or they didn't have the funds to do so.

Covid-19 should teach the lesson that subsistence is not a viable way of running either a business or one's life. All stakeholders will need to take stock and rethink how they will move forward, if they remain able to do so, after the impact of the economic downturn once the pandemic is over. What the future holds is anyone's guess but knowing Thailand, it will be interesting!

Chapter 10
Muay Thai Fighter Glorifcation and Other Anecdotes

Something that perplexes me as much now as it did when I first became involved in the sport, is the glorification of MT fighters/coaches and the tendency to see them as superior to all. This is not restricted to MT alone and is commonly found across the martial arts. The principles of discipline and respect, instilled into students, are integral to martial arts culture. Whilst these are worthy principles, it can lead to a dangerous abuse of power by a minority. Such reverence towards a teacher recently led to the death of a 7-year-old boy in Taiwan.

More commonly in Thailand, it can result in confusion amongst some students as to the amount of leeway a Thai coach should be given. Some students are even prepared to overlook a coach's criminal activities if it suits them to do so. Values held so dearly in their own country are forgotten when in Thailand. I have yet to understand why this is so.

A relatively innocuous example of this was observed when talking to a young student of MT who was anxious to train at a gym in Esaan. He had trained there before and told me that it was such fun there because the trainers were often drunk during the training session. He reported that the trainers started drinking in the early morning and continued throughout the day. I asked him if he would consider going to a gym in his home country if the coaches there behaved in the same way. He gave me a bewildered look and said 'Of course not!' There have, however, been a number occasions when glorification of a trainer/coach has had chilling consequences.

My attention was first drawn to this when I read the *Vice* article by Alexander Reynolds 'RIP Nokweed Davy', written as a celebration of Nokweed's achievements as a fighter. Towards the end of the piece, in a short paragraph, it was mentioned as an aside that Nokweed had used the skills he had learnt as a MT fighter to kill in cold blood a taxi driver he had got into an argument with. Nokweed was known as an awesome leg kicker and it was by kicking the taxi driver in the neck that he killed him. There was not a hint of admonishment in the article. Indeed, the article ended with the following: 'He was more than good. He was much, much more than that.' Can this be right? Nokweed Davy's case is not the only instance where I have seen followers openly offer support to a fighter known to have killed someone in cold blood.

In a country where the judicial system is not as robust as it might be, easy forgiveness sets a dangerous precedent. In Nokweed's case, despite killing someone, he was bailed out of prison by the mafia to fight in a number of lucrative bouts. It could be argued that such a machination engenders successful MT fighters to believe that they are above the law and can do whatever they wish.

On a personal level, my experience of the dangers of this kind of glorification has been in relation to the safety of women training in gyms. Trainers who have been known to commit serious sexual assaults, sometimes rape, continue to be held in high regard by their supporters and often by their peers too. In highly patriarchal societies such as Thailand, often the victim is blamed rather than the perpetrator, making them reluctant to report the crime to the authorities.

Social control is the first level of controlling criminality. Without it, there can be serious repercussions. In the context of MT gyms, perpetrators are often allowed to either remain *in situ* or move to another teaching position, frequently finding other victims.

Funeral and Fundraising Event for Superlek Sorn Esaan

An experience which was interesting, memorable and sombre was Superlek's funeral in Ubon Ratchathani in 2013. Sadly Superlek, known for his heavy punches, died prematurely from sepsis and alcoholism when he was just 44 years old.

Ubon Ratchathani is in the northeast Esaan region of Thailand and was home to the famous Sor Sumalee Gym (SSG). (This was the gym Sumalee Phuket was named after when our training was under the stewardship of Deachkalon Sor Sumalee.) SSG produced many famous fighters of the golden age and Superlek was one of them. Others included Jompoplek, Lamnamoon and Deachkalon.

On hearing of Superlek's death, Deachkalon was keen to return to Ubon Ratchathani for the funeral to pay homage to a fighter who had been a guiding light for him during his younger years. Superlek was approximately twelve years older than Deachkalon. I was invited to accompany Deachkalon to Ubon Ratchathani by the owners of SSG.

Lamnamoon greeted us on arrival at the airport in Ubon. It was not the first time I had met him as I had visited Ubon Ratchathani on several occasions previously. He was a comparable age to Superlek and as training partners they would have been very close to one another. In many respects, Lamnamoon acted as the MT host for the funeral.

Lamnamoon took us to the temple where Superlek was laid for several days prior to his cremation. This provided an opportunity to pay our respects to him as a person and as a fighter. Many people came to do so. Successful MT fighters from rural areas form one of the pillars of their community. Everyone in the neighbourhood knows them, supports them and follows their career. They take enormous pride in their achievements. It is not unusual for up-and-coming fighters to receive a free education, acting as role models and ambassadors for their schools.

The occasion of Superlek's funeral highlighted how close-knit the MT community is. Many MT celebrities from all aspects of the business attended the funeral, including the famous promoter Songchai Rattanasuban, who travelled up from Bangkok. Songchai's attendance at the funeral was a testament to the esteem in which Superlek was held as a MT fighter.

Most of the well-known fighters from the SSG stable attended the funeral. Something that was abundantly clear was that MT had given these ex-fighters a lifetime of career and other opportunities that many youngsters from that region would never have. They were smartly dressed and urbane compared to their peers. At the time Deachkalon had a good position as business partner and Head Trainer with Sumalee Phuket. Lamnamoon had built on his national reputation by becoming a trainer at Evolve Gym in Singapore. This together with burgeoning social media exposure had propelled him into greater international recognition. I am unsure as to what Jompoplek was doing at that time but he certainly appeared to have an air of success about him.

During the cremation ceremony itself, attended by

hundreds of people, Deachkalon was given the honour of performing a wai khru (a dance performed by MT fighters to honour their teachers). Deachkalon was well known for his unique wai khru into which he had woven a part for the khene, a traditional Esaan pipe instrument. During his time as an active fighter, Deachkalon was often referred to as the King of Esaan Dancing. His performance on that day was gracious and full of decorum. It added a distinctive touch of MT to the ceremony uniting mourners in their grief over the premature death of a celebrated fighter.

For me, a particularly macabre aspect of the ceremony was that, unlike a cremation in the UK where the coffin is removed from the sight of the mourners, the coffin was lit before our eyes. Not only that, prior to lighting the flames, men threw tinder into the open coffin and even went in themselves with hatchets. I was frozen to the spot because I couldn't believe what I was witnessing. I have subsequently been told that prior to a cremation in Thailand, the skull is broken to prevent the brain from exploding. I am not sure if this is what was happening to Superlek's body and perhaps it is best not to dwell too deeply on it.

As he died prematurely, there was no provision made for Superlek's wife and family. In all honesty, even if he had had time to prepare, it is unlikely that any provision would have been made. A Thai fighter's early life, divorced from making any decisions for themselves, often leaves them ill-equipped to deal with financial matters later on in life. Many fighters die in poverty, even if they had earned considerable amounts during the peak of their careers.

To support Superlek's family, Lamnamoon organised a fundraising charity event a few months after the champion's death. He asked Sumalee Phuket to assist. Honoured to be asked, we willingly sponsored the travel, accommodation and living costs for Deachkalon, a foreign fighter, and the support team, to travel to Ubon Ratchathani to fight in the promotion. Lamnamoon paid a small fight purse of THB6,000 to each fighter. Orono Por Muang Ubon, also from Ubon Ratchathani but not from SSG, came out of retirement to fight in the show and honour Superlek.

To add to the atmosphere and authenticity of the event, Lamnamoon held it in the stadium in the town of Ubon, where Superlek had fought in his younger days. The problem was that the stadium had not been used for over twenty years. It was a wooden construction that had seen better days. Halfway through the event the electricity failed and at one stage it looked as if the event would have to be abandoned. The organisers managed to create enough light for the fights to go on but the audience spent most of the evening in darkness.

I don't know how many people attended the event but there seemed to be thousands there. The community arrived in droves to support Superlek's family and to relive the days when the old stadium was very much at the centre of what went on in the town. THB400,000 was raised for Superlek's family. Superlek's son, Padsaenlek Sor Sumalee, also fought; unfortunately he lost his fight. I am sure it must have been a great disappointment for him to lose in an event organised to honour his father.

Both of our fighters won their bouts although regrettably, the foreigner received a serious injury to his face that required reconstructive surgery on his return to Phuket. Fortunately he had insurance. The injury did put him out of action for several months though. Foreigners in general are ineligible for free health services in Thailand. Having insurance is something many fighters overlook, often because they are unable to afford it. Doing so can be a costly mistake as promoters themselves are often not insured for the events they hold. Certainly, in this particular case the event organisers did not appear to be in a position to offer assistance.

MT is at the core of Thai culture, particularly amongst poorer communities. The strength of the bonds formed was evident at both the funeral and the charity event held in honour of Superlek's life as a fighter. These bonds would have been formed over many years, more often than not since childhood. It is a real brotherhood. For a foreigner, no matter how well connected they are, it's difficult to be an integral part of this.

Social Media

Using social media for vindictive purposes is very common within the MT community. Social media and online platforms have done a great deal to promote the sport and generate interest in it worldwide. However, the lines between personal use of social media and business/professional use are blurred within this particular community. The sport as a whole would benefit if influencers themselves would use social media in a responsible way to enhance the image of the sport rather than for the wrong sort of point-scoring exercises. Sadly, most of the inappropriate use of social media personally witnessed stems from foreigners rather than Thais.

Leaving a detrimental review of an establishment is often used as a means of 'payback' in the event that things don't go the customer's way. As an American citizen recently found out to his cost, doing this in Thailand can lead you into rather deep waters. This particular person was persistent in writing negative reviews of a hotel in Koh Chang because they would not allow him to consume alcohol purchased off-site in their restaurant without paying a corkage charge. When the avalanche of poor reviews started coming in, the hotel tried without success to resolve the issue amicably. When the American refused to settle matters in this way, the hotel used the Thai defamation laws as the basis for getting the American arrested. He was imprisoned for several days and to avoid court action, he was required to rescind his review with a written public apology. He lost his job in Thailand and subsequently had to leave the country.

There was an occasion where a negative review of a MT gym led to a potentially more sinister outcome. We sponsored a British fighter with little knowledge of his background. He had previously trained at a gym in Bangkok that had been recommended to him. He felt dissatisfied with his experience there and wrote a negative and potentially detrimental blog post reviewing the gym on his departure.

We only became aware of this when trainers from the gym contacted our HT and threatened to take a plane down to Phuket to deal with the fighter. The owner of the gym, who was also a well-known fight promoter, took a more reasoned approach and contacted me personally. He happened to be influential in the MT fraternity. He explained his position clearly and told me that if the fighter did not take his review down he would ensure that the fighter would never have a fight career in Thailand. I believed him.

I spent a considerable amount of time with the fighter explaining the wisdom of taking the review offline if he wanted to continue fighting in Thailand. Eventually, but reluctantly, the fighter agreed to take the review offline. No apology was solicited from him and taking the blog post offline ended the matter.

In fact, several years later this particular fighter achieved considerable acclaim from winning a popular tournament organised by the gym owner/promoter in question. The gym owner/promoter may have harboured a grudge but he was not prepared to let this get in the way of a business decision to have this popular fighter on his show several years later. Unlike Tripadvisor, where the owner of an establishment can respond to a review and also has the last word, it is not possible to do this with a blog post. A one-sided negative opinion by an influencer that remains online unchecked can therefore have long-term detrimental repercussions. Freedom of expression is one thing but deliberately setting out to destroy someone's livelihood is quite another.

Substance Abuse

Thailand has the air of being a country where anything goes. In fact, the reverse is true but what does differ here is enforcement. There are many reasons for this, the main ones being underfunding of public services and the pervading culture of corruption.

Many foreigners are seduced by the apparent laissez-faire attitude that prevails in Thailand. Their lack of awareness of what goes on under the surface can lead them into deep trouble if they break the law.

The drug laws in Thailand are draconian and being caught with even a small amount of a Class C drug can lead to court action, a heavy fine, imprisonment or even deportation. It is illegal to be in possession of mild barbiturates such as Xanax without a prescription. Visitors to Thailand who take such prescription drugs are well advised to be aware of this. They need to carry the prescription with them.

At the time of writing, barbiturate usage in combination with other recreational drugs was on the rise and popular amongst the clubbing fraternity. Obtaining prescription drugs such as Xanax from local pharmacies in Thailand without a prescription was relatively easy for a long time. (More recently, the authorities have put in place measures to prevent this.) In consequence, it was not difficult for partygoers to obtain the barbiturates, making them a popular mood-changing option. As easy as it was to be in illegal possession of these barbiturates, so was being caught by the police.

One of our short-term students found himself in such a position. Whether there were other drugs involved was unknown to me. He was apprehended at a police checkpoint in the area of the island well known for its nightlife. Having no explanation for the drugs he was carrying, he was taken to Patong police station, where he spent the night in a crowded prison cell. As the only English-speaking person amongst a predominantly Burmese group, he felt intimidated and distressed. On the evening he was arrested, he was not able to contact anyone in a position to assist him. He was also told that he would be taken to court where a heavy fine would be levied, following which he would be deported and not allowed to re-enter Thailand for a minimum of ten years. As his family owned a house in Phuket, the threat of not being allowed to re-enter Thailand for a considerable period loomed large for him. Added to this was his concern over how his family, who had some standing in their local community, would respond. In short, he was petrified.

When he was allowed access to a phone after spending an uncomfortable night in the cell, he called me and implored me to do whatever I could to help. As my Thai-language skills were not strong at the time, my staff were sent to do whatever they were able to. This prompted negotiations and he was offered the option of paying a fine of THB200,000 to avoid going to court. The fine had to be paid immediately if this option was chosen. The student had no immediate access to such funds. If he was to get out of the fix he was in, then we were going to need to assist him. Of course, it was difficult for us to do that without knowing that we would be reimbursed. He asked us to contact his brother, who naturally was hugely concerned about him. The brother gave us the reassurances we needed for us to help the student out with the immediate funds.

This student was fortunate that his family had the resources to help him. The system of bribes worked in his favour, although one could argue that it doesn't work in favour of wider society. There will be many Thai nationals as well as immigrants from poor countries who would be unable to buy themselves out of a situation like this.

Anyone visiting Thailand should be aware that in this case, looks do deceive. Despite appearing to be a very carefree society, underneath it all Thailand is a conservative country and anything does not go.

A Family Party

This particular experience happened before I was directly involved in MT. I had, however, already started helping a Thai fighter. It was through him that my daughter and I were invited to the birthday party of a businessman who is prominent and influential within the MT business community (hereafter referred to as Puu Yai).

The party was held on the top floor of a hotel in Patong, which this businessman owned. Our fighter friend assured us that we would be welcome at the family party. It was initially awkward because at that time neither my daughter nor I spoke any Thai. All the other guests were Thai. It was a mixture of other local businessmen and the family of the person whose birthday it was. The wife, children and grandchildren of Puu Yai were amongst the guests.

We were fortunate that we were seated next to a Thai lady who had been educated in the UK and who spoke English fluently. This eased the situation and we had much to talk to her about. I was interested when she said at one stage that it was unusual for the women in the group to have so much to say. She told us that usually in these mixed situations the women took a back seat and didn't talk much. I have since observed this many times. It is also not unusual to see that in large family/friendship groups, the women sit separately from the men. In gatherings like these, it is not unusual for the women not to consume any alcohol, especially older, more traditional women.

We noticed around 9pm that the family members were preparing to leave as well as the lady we had been conversing with. We didn't think too much of it. We stayed, enjoying a beer or two. About half an hour later, we noticed that apart from my daughter and me, no other women remained in the room. Nobody seemed concerned about this. It was with great surprise that we saw around eight well-presented and beautiful hostesses entering via the stairs. They were clearly expected, as the men in the room did not react at all. Almost immediately, the men selected a woman and took them downstairs, presumably to use the hotel's facilities. We decided at this stage that it was probably a good idea to leave. As an introduction to the position of women in Thai culture, this was a baptism of fire.

Business Protocol

When it comes to formality, business protocol in Thailand tends to be one extreme or the other; either far too informal or far too formal.

Suppliers, service providers and even lawyers and accountants like to use the Line app for communication. This in itself is not a problem but persistently using childish emojis to communicate on business matters feels totally inappropriate. It is also frustrating to find that service providers, such as lawyers/accountants, dealing with confidential company information will ignore proper communication channels and discuss these private matters openly with junior staff.

In formal meetings, strict protocols are followed and with little tolerance for anything light-hearted. Something that has surprised me even in formal meetings, is that it is not unusual for introductions not to be made. Apparently, people of importance assume you know who they are and consequently introductions are not needed. It really puts you on the back foot if you have no idea what the position and status of the person you are dealing with is.

This happened to us when we met with representatives of the gym that threatened to sue us over their fighter (see Chapter 8). Not only were we unsure who we were speaking to, but also there was somebody present taking photographs of us without our consent. I requested that photographs not be taken. It became apparent later why they wanted them. When the fighter left that gym, it resulted in a considerable loss of face for the owner. He wanted the photographs to circulate on social media claiming that the meeting represented an apology from Sumalee and the fighter. This was not the case.

In terms of breaking normal business protocol, one meeting in particular stands out. It was in the early stages of setting up the Sumalee business. A meeting was arranged for our directors, the landowners and our lawyer. Our male lawyer arrived with a woman who I assumed was his assistant, although I felt she was inappropriately dressed for that position. The meeting room table had space for only eight people. There were ten participants altogether. I invited the lawyer and his 'assistant', who was never introduced, to sit at the table. This meant that representatives of the landowner were not able to sit at the main table.

When I later discussed the meeting with another lawyer from the law office, I mentioned how strange it was that her male colleague had brought a woman to the meeting but had not introduced her. She asked me to describe her, which I did. Imagine my surprise when I found out that the woman in question was in fact the lawyer's mistress. On finding this out, her code of dress made sense. Bringing the mistress was in itself unsuitable but allowing her to take the place of stakeholders at the meeting table took unprofessionalism to another level.

Business Ambassadors

Over the years since we opened Sumalee, some of our supporters have become ambassadors for the business. This is an informal arrangement. They are people who have enjoyed training with us to such an extent that they want others to have this experience too.

Many of these ambassadors visit us time and time again, getting to know the staff and the fighters (usually sponsored) who train at Sumalee on a long-term basis. On occasions, ambassadors visiting sporadically have been drawn into disputes (usually involving the long-term fighters) without really understanding the background and the dynamics within the gym. More often than not the ambassador only hears one side of the story as poor language skills mean that Thai staff/trainers are unable to put their side forward. This can lead to a lot of tension in the gym, as ambassadors are valuable in promoting the business. Consequently, it's damaging if they get drawn into disputes between fighters and trainers.

Something that was impressed upon me whilst studying for my postgraduate diploma in digital marketing, was that ambassadors are powerful allies but even more powerful if they become enemies. In one particular case, an ambassador who became involved in a dispute between a fighter and a trainer without being aware of the full background then decided to do whatever he could to damage the reputation of the business. He continually made derogatory remarks about the gym on social media, contacted customers and encouraged them not to train with us, and even tried to entice fighters whom we had sponsored for a long time to move to another competitor gym.

This particular ambassador's interest in MT was solely recreational, weight loss being his main goal. He was at a crossroads in his own life and perhaps taking on the issues of others gave him a purpose. He eventually moved on with his life, leaving his passing interest in MT behind. Sadly, he left a mark, making us cautious of people who become too involved in the minutia of what goes on behind the scenes in the business.

Age and Respect in Thai Culture

Age is an important marker of one's place in the community and pervades every aspect of daily life in Thai culture. Respect for one's elders and those of higher social rank is a key determinant of social behaviour.

Age (and social rank) provides order within Thai communities. It is important, not least because forms of address are dependent on whether the person being addressed is older or younger. If someone is older, you should address them as 'Pee' (followed by their Christian name) and a younger person is referred to as 'Nong'.

Almost everything you do or apply for in Thailand requires you to give information about your age. This happens even if age is irrelevant to the matter in hand. For example, when interviewed about my business in Phuket, I am always asked how old I am to set the context. Other more relevant questions such as what is your background, what brought you to this type of business are rarely or, more usually, never asked.

The question about age is always very direct and never disguised by asking, for example, what is your date of birth. Frustratingly too, age is often published in both official and unofficial documents. It appears visibly on documents like house contracts and work permits.

For Thai people age is important not only because it determines the way they address one another but also the way they behave towards each other. Older people command respect whether or not, using our terms of reference, they deserve it. In Thailand, it is expected that you respect what an older person has to say. You must listen and abide by their advice, whether or not you agree with it. Simply because of their age, an older person is regarded as a wiser person.

In a MT gym, the age rule impacts heavily on the running of the business.

Veteran fighter Sylvie von Duuglas-Ittu writes endearingly about how it is important to understand age relativity when it comes to forms of address in a MT gym.

The influence of the age hierarchy pervades much more deeply than most people who visit gyms realise. In particular it creates problems when promotion has been based on merit rather than age. Not following the age rule can upset the natural order within a gym.

At Sumalee, we had made some significant changes to our team, appointing a HT based on merit. There was a feeling of optimism as we believed the changes would have a positive effect on how the team functioned. Imagine my surprise when I received a phone call from another trainer telling me he was on the bus to Bangkok. As he had not given me notice of his departure, I hesitantly asked, 'When are you coming back?' He said, 'I am not coming back.' I was perplexed. I had no idea what the problem was so I asked him. He told me, 'No problem. I am just not coming back!'

It took me some time to uncover what had happened. Thai people are usually reluctant to discuss situations of conflict. They prefer not to say anything. This avoids causing problems for themselves or for others. Getting to the bottom of what goes on in the gym among the Thai staff can consequently be difficult.

In this case, however, the HT was prepared to tell me what had happened. He and the trainer had been discussing which one of them spoke English the best. The HT asserted, quite correctly in fact, that he could speak English better because he had been working with foreigners for longer. However, because the HT was younger than the other trainer, he had offended him by asserting his superior skill. The subordinate felt the HT had shown a lack of respect for his age. Without further ado, he packed his bags and boarded a bus to go home to Bangkok.

On this occasion, we were able to resolve the situation without too much loss of face on behalf of either trainer. We reassured the trainer who left that he was an essential member of the team whom we could not do without. Fortunately, this was enough to persuade him to return. Indeed it was the truth; he was a very valued member of the team.

I was THB4,000 worse off because I had to pay for his return airfare. It was a sharp reminder of the complexities that operate within Thai society. Being the workplace senior and in the right are not sufficient grounds in Thailand for asserting superiority in anything. In Thailand, unless you are the elder, discussions around who is the more knowledgeable are best avoided!

Dominance in a Muay Thai Gym

As in most working environments, hierarchies establish themselves within any MT camp in Thailand. What is different, though, is physical dominance often plays a significant role in determining where a person is in the pecking order.

As far as imposing a structure is concerned, we came to find that offering the position of HT was counterproductive. In our experience, this has led to an abuse of power and confusion amongst the Thai training staff as to who is in overall control of the business. We now give trainers specific roles and we do not use the term Head Trainer.

Natural order can be expressed in unusual ways. 'Testicle grabbing' by dominant males happens a lot in MT camps. It is something that foreign males find quite threatening. However, it is not meant to be threatening at all. It is an expression of one's 'place' relative to another in the gym. Thai trainers do it a lot to youngsters in the gym. It can lead to great discomfiture on behalf of parents of children from overseas. Indeed, one parent threatened to involve the police if a particular trainer continued to grab the testicles of his son. I feared he would not have received the reaction he would expect from the police, as in Thai society, this behaviour was entirely normal. Instead, we dealt with the problem internally by making the trainer aware of the discomfiture he was causing the parent.

Dominance is sometimes expressed in more unpleasant ways. Many people may have witnessed a young Thai fighter being hit by his Thai trainer if his performance is under par. It is often seen at the stadiums. Westerners find this shocking and offensive. For the Thais, however, it is normal and is seen as a way of showing who is in control.

Another thing that Westerners feel uncomfortable with, and it is certainly discouraged, are instances of trainers putting students in 'their place'. It is unpleasant to see and fortunately it only relates to a minority of Thai trainers. Although it doesn't make it right, knowing where this behaviour comes from at least helps to understand it. The trainer is doing what was done to him when he was young. Some trainers see it as their duty to remind a student who overestimates his ability that there is always someone bigger and stronger than them around. They believe this makes the student better prepared for going into the ring.

A Cautionary Tale

I add this anecdote as many foreigners who come to stay in Thailand on a long-term basis get caught out in the way. By telling the story, it is my hope that forearmed is forewarned and others will not be caught out in the same way.

Before settling semi-permanently in Thailand, we had visited frequently for ten years. We always stayed at the same hotel in the north of the island that was remote from the mainstream of activity in Phuket. Rather than hire a car when we needed to go out, we used the same driver for many years.

This particular driver has a business offering car rental too. When I came to Thailand initially for a year, I rented a car from him. He offered a deal where if I paid for ten months in advance, he would give me twelve months' rental. I realise now that my advance payment was used as a down payment for the car, the remainder of which was to be paid off over a period of at least five years. At this stage, this matter was of no concern to me.

Several months later, the driver came to see me and asked if he could borrow money from me. He explained that he wanted to start a laundry business and that he already had a hotel client for the business. He told me that in Thailand it takes a long time for the banks to agree to a loan and that if he wasn't able to service the hotel customer quickly, he would lose the opportunity. He reassured me that as soon as the bank agreed to his application for the loan, he would repay the money. By that time, I had known him for eleven years. I knew his wife, his parents and other family members, so I trusted him and lent him the money. It was a substantial sum.

By the end of the year, he still had not repaid the money. When I decided to stay in the country on a semi-permanent basis, we came to an agreement where the car would be mine in lieu of his paying off the loan. When we made this agreement, I was still unaware that the car had been purchased with a five-year finance agreement.

I only became aware of this when, to my horror, I was out at a local restaurant with my staff and some bailiffs came in with a clipboard looking for the owner of my car. I had no idea what was happening as the conversation with my staff was in Thai. It transpired that the two men had come to repossess the car because the repayments had not been made for many months.

After prolonged negotiations and many telephone calls, my driver of old reassured the company tasked with repossessing the car that he would cover the backlog of payments.

Now that I have been here longer, I have realised that it often happens that purchasers are unable to make their monthly payments. In these situations, the car is sometimes relocated to another part of the country, making it more difficult to trace. To overcome this, finance companies (usually banks) employ companies to track down the cars and repossess them.

Despite his reassurance, my errant driver did not restart the payments. The attempt to repossess the car described was the first of three with the final one being successful. One of our trainers had used the car to take two fighters to a weigh-in at a stadium in Patong. A repossession company came, the trainer didn't know whom to contact, so he allowed them to take the car.

That was the last I ever saw of the car or of the money lent to the driver. When I talked to him about it, his rationale was that I (and people like me) were very fortunate in that we come from a country where it is possible to accrue wealth. This is indeed true. However, that doesn't mean it is justifiable to break someone's trust by asking them to help with a loan knowing that there was no means to repay the money.

Informal borrowing is common in Thailand because most people do not have the collateral to secure a loan through more formal channels. I am frequently asked by our staff to help them with small loans. It is a credit to them that not one of them has ever failed to repay the loan. When it comes to other requests for loans, I have learnt my lesson and I don't do it.

During my time here, I have been cheated on a number

of other occasions too, some of which have been described in this book. I have also been burgled on two occasions. The circumstances of the burglary lead me to believe that both times the miscreant had direct connections with me or my business. On the second occasion, all my jewellery collection, which included many sentimental items, was taken.

Prior to the Covid-19 pandemic, my personal goal was not to leave Thailand until I had built up at least enough money from the business to replace all that had been taken from me through the burglaries and by being duped. During the long period when international borders were been closed, the business has suffered greatly, depleting reserves. This goal now seems much harder to achieve than it did before.

Chapter 11
A Change in Direction

The original concept for Sumalee was a traditional MT gym. We chose the location and built it with this in mind. In 2011 there were only three MT gyms of note in Phuket: Rawai Muay Thai (which was the first MT gym in Phuket designed to cater for the overseas market); Tiger Muay Thai and Sinbi Muay Thai (both off-shoots of Rawai Muay Thai). Phuket Top Team had only just opened and Phromthep Muay Thai had recently closed because of an acrimonious dispute between the Australian and Thai owners. Since 2011 innumerable gyms catering for the overseas market have opened, although quite a few came and went over a relatively short time period.

By 2016, MT gyms catering primarily for the overseas market had become a crowded space. Not only was the competition increasing, but the amount of money being invested in these gyms was increasing too. AKA Thailand in the Rawai area was a prime example of such heavy investment. To retain their market share, the more enlightened gym owners began to diversify. Most went further down the martial arts route, adding disciplines such as MMA, Western Boxing and Brazilian Jujitsu. Tiger Muay Thai, Phuket Top Team and AKA Thailand, three of the biggest gyms at that time, all diversified in this direction.

At Sumalee we found ourselves at a crossroads too. The

gym had been open for five years. Superficially the gym appeared to be very successful and, in many respects, we were doing well. We'd certainly established a strong reputation for training and developing foreign fighters. A number of well-known Thai fighters had either trained with us or fought under our name including Payakdam, Lerdsila, Yodkhun and Yodbuangam. We'd employed a number of well-known trainers too, including Deachkalon, Parinya, Payakdam, Yodbuangam and Kaenchai Fairtex.

(Incidentally, during the period of writing this book, Kaenchai Fairtex died suddenly and prematurely of a heart attack during his sleep. He was only 38 years old and leaves behind two young children (3 and 8 years at the time of his death). Representing the plight of many Muay Thai champions, he died in poverty. His elderly mother is left to bring up the children without a breadwinner in the family. Sumalee has set up an ongoing fund and the money raised will be used to contribute to the education of his children.)

Our team was working almost around the clock to push the boundaries. Typically, MT gyms open at 7.30am and close at 6pm. They are open six days a week. Added to this, during the evenings the team were required to take fighters to fight in local stadiums, sometimes three times a week.

At least once a month it was necessary to take fighters to bigger promotions elsewhere in Thailand over a weekend. Long journeys would be involved and at least two nights in a hotel. Since none of the fighters, Thai or foreign, had their own transport, it came down to the management team to assist with ferrying fighters around. Fight purses were usually meagre, ruling out the option of hiring a company to provide the transportation. The shows were often in remote locations too. On several occasions, we drove fighters down to the most southerly province of Thailand (Narathiwat) and even over the border into the Malaysian provinces of Kedah, Kelantan and Langkawi. Drives such as these took around twelve hours, often through hostile territory patrolled by the army, located there as protection against separatist insurgents in Southern Thailand.

Make no mistake about it: running a fully-fledged MT gym is an all-encompassing means of making a living. The pressures are enormous because an owner is not just running a business but is responsible for the smooth running of a tight-knit but disparate community. The content of the previous chapters will have made this abundantly clear.

Of course, one of the greatest challenges in any business is for it to be financially viable. A couple of things became clear to me during the first five years of running the Sumalee business. Firstly, whilst we were working long hours and making headlines, we were not in complete control of our own business. Secondly, whilst we never ran at a loss, we were not building any reserves that would help us through a troubled period. Of course, at that time, I had not anticipated a world pandemic, which would in 2020/21 strangle the life out of most tourism-related businesses in Phuket.

Numerous factors were impinging on our ability to be in full control of the business and ergo, our income. We were too subject to the vagaries of promoters, head trainers and fighters to be able to consistently plot our own course. Over the previous five years there had been many ups and downs, the shockwaves of which were sometimes quite traumatic.

It was time to change. We even considered completely changing course and moving away from MT altogether. Fortunately, we were able to find another way.

From the outset I had set my sights on offering our customers nutritious food to support high-intensity training. I wanted the gym to be known as much for the quality of our food as for the quality of our training. Our path to achieving this goal was wobbly initially as we were reliant on the whims of local untrained Thai staff that came and went with more frequency than I would care to mention. We were struggling to find consistency and quality in this area so Rhian decided she would like to manage the catering side of the business herself. From that time, we went from strength to strength and the quality of the nutritional support we were able to offer set us apart from much of the competition.

My son, Sam, who later went on to become a fully qualified nutritionist, indulged his interest in this field by providing nutritional guidance and support to the fighters. Together with Rhian, he designed meal plans to help them with weight cuts and gave them guidance on how to lose weight safely. We even had a number of patrons, keen to help the fighters, sponsor their meal plans on several occasions. All our fighters at that time knew what was and was not advisable to do to achieve weight cuts for fights.

We started offering training packages that included a meal plan selected from a menu designed to support a high-intensity MT training regime. The packages have become a not-insignificant part of our success as a gym business. At any one time, up to 80% of people training with us would have chosen the meal plan/package option, which is testament to the success of the programme.

With what had become a renowned training programme and the right nutritional support, Sumalee was headed in the mindfulness direction; it seemed an obvious path to me. I had been much influenced by a trip Rhian and I made to the Power of Now Oasis yoga studio in Bali. Theirs was an iconic studio made of bamboo with a ground-floor relaxation area and an upper level for yoga practice. Unfortunately, when we returned to Phuket, we were unable to find a contractor to create a studio in this style. Instead we opted for a traditional Thai style opened-sided shala that has a beauty of its own.

Adding yoga, in a dedicated space designed to enhance the benefits of practice, gave us something truly unique. No other gym in Phuket had done this, neither at that time nor since. Since witnessing the success of our programme, a few gyms have tried to introduce yoga sessions using the MT gym space, perhaps not understanding that to achieve a mindful state, the environment needs to be conducive to it.

The addition of a daily yoga programme in our beautiful yoga shala changed the fortunes of the business almost overnight. Rhian took full responsibility for this aspect of the business, qualifying as a yoga instructor to do so. As hinted previously, I had courted the idea of moving away from MT completely once the yoga shala was built. However, the appeal of the joint programme was such that to do so would have been a retrograde move. We opened the yoga shala in September 2016 and by Christmas our room occupancy levels increased so that they were consistently near 100% in high season and around 70% in low season.

By happenstance, we had found a winning formula. Sumalee became a place where people could nourish body and soul in a holistic way that was unavailable in competitor MT gyms.

The addition of a massage shala in 2018, built in the same style as the yoga shala, completed the circle and cemented Sumalee's position as a place where students could both push themselves to the limit and nurture body and soul.

Introducing the yoga programme had many unanticipated benefits for the business overall. It radically changed our customer base. Not unexpectedly it attracted more women to come and train with us, making it a less hostile and intimidating environment for beginners to train in. Many new customers came to us for the yoga first and foremost but as a result of their experience at Sumalee 'found' MT, bringing more people into the sport. It had long been my belief that by focusing marketing primarily on fighters, MT gyms were not only limiting their market but were inhibiting the growth of the sport outside the fight community.

As Thailand makes the transition to a developing economy, opportunities for employment are increasing. Families from poor rural communities are less inclined to want their offspring to become a MT fighter in the knowledge that not only is it a hard life but that it is a life in which they have little control over their own destiny.

An additional factor that may be affecting recruitment into the sport stems from the growth of smartphone ownership amongst all levels of Thai society. Internationally, the growth of smartphone ownership has stimulated interest in the sport. On the contrary, however, locally it means that Thai people especially are exposed to a wealth of online media reports highlighting some of the more unsavoury aspects of the sport, as well as other negative news stories on a regular basis.

For example, the assault of a referee by armed assailants outside Lumpinee stadium, leading to the slaying of a security guard, was widely reported in Thai media in 2017. More recently, it was widely reported that the high-profile Thai fighter Porsarnae had shot an acquaintance in an apparently unprovoked attack.

In another hit to the image of MT, the decision by the army owners of Lumpinee stadium to go ahead with a show they were asked to cancel was attributed to the first wave of Covid-19 to hit Thailand.

All this would have done nothing to improve the image of MT in Thailand and may well diminish any desire to be a part of it.

At the time of writing, the impact of Covid-19 on the MT community in Thailand has been enormous. MT is potentially one of the businesses most affected. Gyms all over Thailand were forced to close for three months at the beginning of Covid-19 in March 2020. Gyms in the Bangkok area were forced to close again in December 2020 and January 2021, and in March 2021 gyms nationwide were required to close for six weeks. A further closure was imposed in July/August 2021. During the periods of closure, no training was allowed.

Lumpinee stadium has been closed for over a year already. Rajadamnern opened for a brief period then closed again. Max Muay Thai stadium has apparently closed not to reopen again. All the local stadiums in tourist hubs such as Phuket and Koh Samui have been closed since the beginning of the pandemic.

Since the time span of active fighting is relatively short, this means that the consequences of being unable to bring on fighters for what will probably turn out to be at least two years will be tremendously detrimental in the long term to the MT business community. In order for the MT business to survive in Thailand, therefore, expanding the scope outside the fight scene has become even more paramount because of Covid-19.

Media Channels

Changing direction gave us a unique proposition but a further step was needed to use this as a tool for growing the business. Online marketing had always been a strength of the business, and much of this was thanks to Mike Davis, who joined us early in the business's genesis.

Mike was a UK friend of my son and we had known him

for many years. He put a post on Facebook in 2011 asking if anyone had any ideas as to how he could change the direction of his life. Realising at an early stage that the task of running all aspects of our business was greater than I had anticipated, I gave him a call and asked him to come over to Thailand to join our team. Mike must be given enormous credit for setting up the foundations of our social media channels. At the time, I was unaware of the many hours he must have spent generating engagement on our channels.

Mike's content creation was so professional and engaging that it attracted two sponsors, Sandee Thailand and Ultim8 Fightwear from Hong Kong. We owe both of these sponsors an enormous debt of gratitude. Sandee Thailand has provided for many years all our gym and trainer boxing equipment. Paul Hickman, who owns the company, has always responded favourably to any requests we have made. Sunny Coelst, who owns Ultim8, has similarly been generous in her support, providing much of the fightwear for our trainers and fighters.

Perhaps Mike's biggest achievement was setting up the YouTube channel from our inception. This means we have a comprehensive library of all our fights. At the time of writing, subscription to our YouTube channel has burgeoned to over 41,000. Our videos have received over nine million views. Most of the videos are fight videos providing a permanent record for both the gym and for the fighters who fought under our name.

One of the most popular videos on the channel, Muay Thai Baby, with just under half a million views at the time of writing, was created by Mike and is symbolic of the ethos of the gym. We have always tried to be original, coming up with our own business ideas to set ourselves apart from what is now a hugely crowded space.

YouTube is an important social media channel in respect

to MT. The platform has had a fundamental influence in growing interest and involvement in the sport. It made what is essentially a Thai sport based in Thailand accessible all over the world. Fans can follow what is happening (often as it happens now with Facebook Live) in a way they never could before.

Digitalisation generally has had a huge positive impact on awareness and involvement in MT. There has been an upsurge of interest in the sport. In July 2021, Muay Thai and its global governing body have been fully recognised by the International Olympic Committee.

It is anticipated that huge benefits will be accrued as a result, especially with regard to standards of monitoring and professionalism within the sport, which in turn will improve the image of the sport.

Although MT can be traced back to the sixteenth century, the proliferation of businesses offering MT training to international students has been a relatively recent phenomenon. Rawai Muay Thai, the pioneer in this field, opened its doors to international students in 2003. By 2009 there were approximately five major MT schools in Phuket. Prior to 2020 and the forced closure of some gyms because of the economic impact of Covid-19, there were at least twenty-four MT gyms in Phuket. The overall value of this business sector in Phuket is not documented but the increasing popularity of fitness vacations is recognised within the travel industry internationally.

The rise in popularity of Muay Thai training has run in parallel to the growth in internet penetration globally and in Thailand. In 2003 internet penetration in Thailand was estimated to be 9%; in 2009 it was 20%; in 2016 it was 42%; and in 2020 it was 75%. A significant proportion of the growth in internet access in Thailand can be attributed to the growth in smartphone ownership, which in 2021 is estimated to be around 75% of the population.

The inevitable outcome of increased internet penetration is a corresponding growth in social media usage. At the beginning of 2021, an estimated 64% of the Thai population use Facebook.

Typically, most gyms did not have a website, let alone a Facebook page (this channel was launched in 2004). Indeed, some traditional MT schools still do not have a website. Twitter was launched in 2006 and Instagram in 2010. YouTube was launched in 2005 and, of all the social platforms; the MT community adopted it the earliest. Tiger Muay Thai in Phuket can be accredited with taking the lead with respect to YouTube and all other digital channels. Their digital reach far outstretches that of any other gyms in Phuket and probably in Thailand as a whole. The successful gyms in Thailand all now realise the importance of online marketing and have a strong digital footprint.

Depth of knowledge amongst enthusiasts about what's going on in the sport is unprecedented. Compared to foreign reporters/influencers, Thai people involved in the sport have been slow adopters when it comes to publishing information online. Having grown up with the sport, it is possible that they don't appreciate either the importance of documenting what's happening or the level of interest there is in it internationally. Authors and journalists such as American Matt Lucas, based in Bangkok for five years, do a wonderful job of keeping international audiences informed about what is happening on the Muay Thai scene in Thailand, and everything of note is now documented.

For foreign-owned MT gyms and all tourism-related businesses, the online revolution with the corresponding growth in social media channels and usage has provided unprecedented opportunities. In the past, prior to arriving, visitors to Thailand were only able to access limited information about the country they were visiting. When they arrived, they were usually channelled along pathways set up between transport providers and local suppliers.

Indeed, when we first opened Sumalee the marketing advice we received locally was to take trays of Coca-Cola to local taxi stands to introduce ourselves. The taxi drivers were seen as having the most influence on where visitors to the island went. In return for directing visitor traffic to them, business owners paid (and often still do) handsome commission to the taxi drivers. This of course meant that the customer was paying much more for the services/goods they received than they actually needed to. In 2010 at the previous gym I invested in, we frequently found that our students were being diverted at the point of entry away from us to another gym on the island, which paid commission to the taxi drivers for bringing customers in. As no system for paying a deposit online was in place, there was no financial penalty for going elsewhere even though a room had been held for them. One of the first things we did on my entering the business was to introduce a system where customers paid a deposit to reserve a room. This sealed their commitment to the gym and prevented them from being persuaded to go to another gym once they arrived here.

Now people get their information and make their reservations before arriving in the country. If anything, it has tipped the balance in favour of those businesses that recognise the importance of digital marketing. These tend to be foreign-owned businesses, which usually have a more advanced digital capability and understanding enabling them to achieve better reach.

In 2015 Mike, who had done the groundwork on all our digital channels, had to return to the UK for personal reasons. This placed us in a difficult position as finding a local replacement with the right expertise was challenging. Being unable to find the right expertise locally and the additional costs of employing overseas personnel (mainly associated with obtaining the required visa and work permit) are factors that inhibit many SMEs in Thailand from achieving their growth potential.

Recognising the importance of digital marketing, I signed myself up for a postgraduate diploma in digital marketing. It was an online course offered by the Digital Marketing Institute based in Dublin, Ireland. It was quite a challenge after so many years of being out of further education and definitely required a gearing-up of brain activity. In all honesty, it was more difficult than I expected. Further education has changed considerably in the years since my time at university when free thinking and creativity were the magic ingredients leading to success. These days, everything is so prescribed and formulaic. However, I obtained the qualification and certainly felt that it was an investment worth making. More than anything else, it gave me the confidence to get behind the scenes of our digital marketing strategy and boost our website with search engine optimisation (SEO).

It encouraged us to invest in our blogging activity. Blog posts have an evergreen value compared to volume-based media that stop delivering value as soon as the campaign investment ends. Similarly, the life span of a social media post is short-lived. With a blog post, however, you can access unreachable prospects, equipping them with every tool and piece of information they need. In doing this, the blog will become an annuity that matures and delivers far and above the original investment. With this knowledge, we invested in the services of a blog post content provider, Will Howell of Copper Milk Creative. This represented a change of course in our marketing strategy that had previously focused predominantly on social media.

Over two years, Will wrote twenty-eight blog posts for us. These blog posts brought over 65,000 views to the website so far. Since the publishing of the blog posts, the monthly traffic to the website has doubled and the traffic volume has been retained over the Covid-19 period.

Bill Gates once said 'content is king'. As one of the richest men on the planet, a philanthropist and the man who co-founded Microsoft, his words carry some weight.

If measured in volume of traffic, financial investment in the postgraduate diploma (it cost approximately £3,000 in 2017) as well as the blog posts certainly paid dividends. Together with Rhian who latterly managed our social media channels, we were able to steadily grow our digital footprint.

Chapter 12

The Unexpected Joys of Owning a Muay Thai Gym in Thailand

Prior to living in Thailand, I had travelled widely both for business and for pleasure. I never had the opportunity to spend an extended period in any country, which limited my awareness of what lies beneath the surface. The period of my travel coincided with the rapid globalisation of the world's major consumer brands. Wherever one went in the world one would see a McDonald's, Nike shops and corporate hotels. I was beginning to feel that travel was overrated. What I failed to appreciate was that whilst superficially things were beginning to look the same all over the world, underneath it all the dynamics of how each country operated were fundamentally different; politically, culturally, socially and economically. Spending such a prolonged period of time in a country such as Thailand has helped me to understand and appreciate this.

This book has outlined the many challenges of building our business in Thailand, with a strong focus on the MT fraternity. The process of building the business has undoubtedly been fraught with many unanticipated tests of our resolve to continue. I have often related that building the Sumalee business has been a culmination of all my life skills: upbringing in a Welsh mining valley town (where incidentally 'Pride of Wales' famous boxer Joe Calzaghe spent his formative years), education, business and financial acumen, parenting and psychology. On more than one occasion, the option to pack up and go has felt vastly appealing.

Nevertheless, growing the Sumalee business has brought with it considerable opportunity for development, for my offspring and myself, and has been so rewarding. It gave me the opportunity to build a business alongside my daughter. It has supported us and allowed me to follow my long-held desire to live and work in Asia for an extended period. Many have the dream of being able to do this but relatively few are able to realise it..

Owning the gym has changed the course of my life and that of my children. Sam expanded his interest in nutrition as a result of assisting the fighters with weight cuts during a stint working with us. With his first degree in Digital Music and Sound Technology, Sam was able to return to university and complete a degree in Nutrition. Through a contact made at Sumalee, he has gone on to become Head of Nutrition working for a major fitness brand in Hong Kong. Rhian has qualified as a Thai-language simultaneous interpreter and has gone on to pursue a career in international aid.

Idyllic Environs

The weather in Thailand is a huge bonus to living here. When you wake up every morning and the weather is warm with the sun shining on at least 80% of occasions, it brings a different feel to the working day. Everything feels better in the sunshine and problems associated with the day-to-day running of the business are no exception. At the end of each day there is the added bonus of being able to enjoy some of the best sunsets in the world.

Thailand's natural environment is stunningly scenic and varied. The longer I stay here, the more I appreciate the extent of what it has to offer. Both the coastal areas and the interior have unparalleled beauty and much of the natural environment is unspoiled. It is reported that Thailand has approximately 1,430 islands, many of which have never been developed at all, let alone for tourism purposes. Being able to live near the sea and beautiful beaches is very much coveted. There is no shortage of either in Phuket and this significantly enhances quality of life here.

About a tenth of all animal and bird species on the planet call Thailand home. To put that into perspective, Thailand has more birds than Europe and America combined. The country has 1,500 species of the orchid, the national flower of Thailand, one of the most exotic and exquisite flowers in the world.

There is a tendency to think that Thailand is drowning from the pressures of tourism. It is true that some areas have suffered unduly in this respect. However, even well-established tourist hubs, such as Phuket, still have large swathes of interior untouched by tourism or indeed human habitation of any kind.

Thailand has a population of approximately 69 million. In population terms, this makes it a similar size to the UK. However, Thailand's land is twice the size of that of the UK (513,120 square kilometres versus 242,495 sq. km).

Thailand is made up of seventy-six provinces. So far I have visited approximately thirty-six of them. A goal of mine is to visit all seventy-six whilst I live here permanently. Although some of the provinces I have visited have been for the purpose tourism, many others have been as a result of my involvement in the MT business. MT has given me the reason and opportunity to experience places few visitors to Thailand, whether long-term residents or tourists, ever get to see. MT has shown me just how much Thailand has to offer and how little there is to fear from going off the beaten track.

During the times I personally accompanied fighters outside of Thailand, I had the honour of travelling in a motorcade on two occasions. The first was when our fighters were on a promotion in Kota Bharu in Malaysia and the second was when Thai Fight did a promotion in Ho Chi Minh City in Vietnam. I remember many years ago witnessing a presidential motorcade in Washington, DC. Bill Clinton was the president at the time. The motorcades I experienced were not on the scale of a presidential one, but the feeling of exclusivity and importance was very much present nevertheless. A unique experience.

Culture and Language

Wherever I have been in Thailand, I have always been received hospitably. It is normal in Thai culture to show concern for someone else's comfort and personal welfare. No matter how little they have, a Thai person is always willing to share their food with you. If they are eating when you visit or approach them, they will ask you to join them at the table. A normal greeting for a Thai person is 'Have you eaten already?' When a Thai person meets you, they are much more interested in knowing this than what one thinks about the weather.

Living in Thailand for so long has enabled me to get closer to fulfilling another lifelong aspiration, which is to become proficient in a second language. I studied French for many years in school and well into my adult life. Never having lived in France though, I was never immersed in the language. For those of us who are not gifted in learning another language, this is a necessity to progress. I started learning Thai during my first year in the country. This was stimulated mainly because Rhian (who is gifted in languages) attained proficiency quickly. As a result, whenever we were in the company of Thai people, it was difficult for me to join in the conversation.

In the early days I learnt the language phonetically. This enabled me to gain a basic level of proficiency. Without being able to read the language, and fully recognise the sounds, my progress was impeded. Downtime during the Covid-19 pandemic has afforded me the opportunity to go back to basics and start learning to read and write Thai. The task of doing this has been like a puzzle, the nearer I get to solving it, the more I am able to see.

I now have the confidence to engage local people in a conversation. Although at this stage I only understand approximately 50% of what they say, these interactions are giving me a deeper understanding of the society, politics and the culture. Having an understanding of the way a language is structured provides much insight into how people within that culture think.

Thailand is predominantly a Buddhist country; however, it's important not to forget that a significant proportion of the population is Muslim. Whilst the overall percentage of Muslims is Thailand is approximately only 5%, in the south of Thailand generally one in four Thai people are Muslim, according to the 2015 census. In Phuket, the proportion is approximately one in five. Such a mix of religions and beliefs is what makes living here both interesting and challenging. To negotiate life successfully, particularly business life, you have to understand both Buddhism and Islam.

Despite living here for twelve years already, much of what I find here is still perplexing to me. In many respects, it is easier for me to understand the Muslim philosophy as it is based on a religion. This is something I can relate to because of my own upbringing as a Christian. Buddhism is a way of living and strongly influences how the majority of Thai people act and think. For the visitor to a Buddhist country, there are many charms, not least of which in Thailand is visiting one of the 35,000 temples scattered across the country. An essential component of Buddhism is mindfulness or living in the moment. Whilst this approach to life has many merits, it can lead to frustrations for foreigners doing business here. Coming from a different business culture, it takes many years for foreigners to get used to the much slower pace of working here. To survive, it's the foreigner who needs to change by becoming more relaxed.

Feeling Welcomed

In common with wider Thai society, I have found the MT community in most part to be open and welcoming. Attaining a deeper and more lasting connection, however, is difficult for a foreigner to achieve. In Thai culture, children are taught from an early age that the most important people are their immediate family circle and the slightly wider radius of their immediate community, however that may be defined. As foreigners, we do not fall into these circles that define how Thai people engage with others.

A significant appeal of MT for many followers must certainly be the ease of access to the superstars of the sport. There are no apparent barriers. Through our involvement and support of Thai Fight and other promotions, it was not unusual to join the table of the well-known and accomplished fighters of the time such as Petchboonchu, Sudsakorn, Saiyok, Saenchai and others. Indeed, to have bought and managed for a short period one of the world's best-known MT fighters,

Saenchai, is an unimaginable honour and a unique experience. This is the epitome of what MT has given me. It has been the chance to have experiences outside the kind of normal daily existence of most people's lives.

As a gym owner, with only a few exceptions, I have been very much welcomed into the MT community and treated with respect. The contribution our gym has made is recognised and appreciated. Given that I am a woman, had no specific background in MT and possessed poor Thai-language skills, especially early on, this is a credit to the community.

The Exhilaration

Many friends and acquaintances have questioned why I became involved with MT, known as one of the most brutal of martial arts. There is no escaping the fact that it is a brutal sport. Paradoxically though, it is also a beautiful sport if executed at its best. Scoring in MT rewards fighters for balance, effectiveness and composure. The skills needed to win are a metaphor for life too. When a Thai fighter goes into a fight, he aims to score just enough points to win. During the course of the fight a respectful fighter will be keeping a mental tally of their score and will only want to score just enough to get ahead. This is why you will often see, towards the end of a bout, fighters circling the ring avoiding further combat. Anyone who has witnessed this ritual at the closing minutes of a fight will know that there is an element of brinksmanship involved, where each fighter wants to convince referees and gamblers that they are the winner. The fighters know what the score is and if one is too far ahead for the other to catch up, they do not wish to inflict further damage on their opponent.

The nuances of the MT scoring system can be confusing.

Those who don't understand it will often be left wondering why a fighter lost when they were throwing more punches or was generally busier. Punches score lower than kicks in MT and if they are not effective, even though a fighter's work rate is high, their scoring will be low. Despite having been involved in the sport for twelve years now, I am often left confused myself as to whether our fighter is in front or not. It sometimes feels like alchemy to me and there certainly is an element of this.

As in any competitive sport, watching is exciting. Especially if you are watching it live. A gym owner is completely immersed in the process from start to finish. The gym owner is ultimately responsible for choosing which fighters to sponsor or to fight under the gym's name. They are also responsible for ensuring the correct training regime is put in place to support the fighter. Where weight cuts are required, they are ultimately responsible for their fighter's welfare. It is in their best interests that weight cuts are overseen and fighters are properly supported during this time. Having invested so many resources and so much energy into the process, witnessing how this translates into performance in the ring is massively adrenaline inducing. An additional bonus to being a gym owner is you are always able to get one of the best seats in the house, ringside.

There are many media reports in existence as to how gambling and drug abuse are impacting the sport. Certainly gambling has unfairly influenced the outcome for Sumalee fighters on a number of occasions. On a personal level, however, I have always steered well clear from this side of the sport. In Thailand, the antics of the gamblers add frenzy and excitement in a stadium. Gamblers will often leave their place to crowd the fighter's corner between rounds, giving them advice on how to win. Most are extremely knowledgeable on fight strategy. Watching a Muay Thai fight in other countries often feels sterile compared to this.

Building a Community

Over the years since Sumalee opened its doors and sponsored fighters, many have become well known internationally. Our online expertise was as much responsible for achieving this as everything else we offered them, including training, financial support, housing, equipment and apparel. To play a role in helping people achieve their dreams has been a worthwhile, if not always fully appreciated, pursuit.

Located in a non-tourist area, Sumalee has enabled the local community to prosper. Our staff live in the local community and rent houses from local landlords. Our customers patronise local shops, restaurants and amenities. We now have a well-known Thai restaurant positioned immediately behind the gym. This restaurant is so well regarded that when the Prime Minister visited Phuket to assess the economic impact of the Covid-19 crisis during the latter half of 2020, he ate there. The proximity of Sumalee would have been a factor influencing the decision to open the restaurant there.

With the support of many of our international customers, during the Covid-19 pandemic we have been able to help the local community, particularly migrant workers, by regularly donating food packs. We also have a programme where underprivileged children in the community can train in MT or practice yoga free of charge. Many local children use our facilities, especially the swimming pool, almost every day.

The income and expertise derived from owning the gym have enabled us to help the wider MT community too. When we renew equipment at the gym, the used equipment is either sent to local gyms in Phuket or shipped to a gym in Surin, Esaan, which one of our trainers is closely associated with. Additionally, we have been able to provide some support to the Wor Watthana gym, also in Esaan, where Frances and Boom Watthanaya aim to use MT as a tool to give opportunity to children born into poverty.

Of all the joys of owning the gym, probably the greatest has been building a worldwide community of supporters. For many of our guests, training at Sumalee has been a life-changing experience. MT training is very intense and some students have discovered a resolve they did not know they had. Some of our customers have used their time training at Sumalee to heal from broken relationships, drug/alcohol addiction, anxiety, depression or mental illness. We did not foresee this when we opened but we are hugely pleased that this has been an incidental outcome.

Friendships have been formed at Sumalee that have lasted for years. Through Facebook and other social media posts, I frequently see past guests communicating and sometimes meeting up long after they were introduced at Sumalee.

Many students wear their Sumalee T-shirts on return to their home country or when vacationing. My son who works in Hong Kong regularly contacts me to tell me he has seen someone there wearing a Sumalee T-shirt. We've even had a previous guest contact us to let us know they met another Sumalee alumni in South America. To know that the name of your business is scattered across the globe generates an enormous feeling of satisfaction.

The range and breadth of students who have trained at Sumalee have been wide. Whilst the majority of our customers have been between the ages of 20 and 45, we have catered for the full range of ages, from all walks of life. Sumalee has trained well-known singers, comedians, actors, private jet pilots, commercial pilots, successful business people, doctors, nurses etc. They have travelled from all over the world to train with us. One of the greatest pleasures of owning the gym is without doubt that many of these have become personal friends. Rhian and I now have the possibility of travelling extensively across the world in the knowledge that wherever we go, we will receive a welcome from someone we know there.

When thinking about all that the sport has given me, it is important for me not to lose sight of the fact that there is an unsavoury side to the sport, which has been touched on in this book. Having been exposed to this during my early years of involvement in the business, I was able to make the decision to walk away from those aspects that didn't sit comfortably with me. I was able to choose my own way and come up with my own formula that was in accord with my values. I remain committed to retaining MT at the core of our business.

To say that the experience has been life changing is an understatement. Would I do it all again? I certainly would. However, I would choose to do it again knowing what I now know to get to where I want to be with much less heartache.

Chapter 13

The Worldwide Covid-19 Pandemic and the Future

I started documenting my experiences of being involved in a MT business in Thailand in April 2020, near the beginning of the worldwide Covid-19 pandemic. Little did I expect that well over a year later we would still be in its grips. With the rollout of the vaccinations, there is some light at the end of the tunnel. Nevertheless, at the time of writing this final chapter (July 2021), Thailand is in its third and most concerning wave of the spread of Covid-19.

The threat posed by Covid-19 was beginning to have an effect on our business at the end of December 2019. Rumours of a deadly virus in Wuhan, China, were emerging. These rumours were substantiated by media reports. At that time, Covid-19 was seen as something that was happening elsewhere and of no immediate relevance to us elsewhere in the world. Like most businesses here in Thailand, however, we took the precaution of not accepting guests who had visited China within three months previously.

Occupancy rates were slowly starting to decline and by early February 2020, concern about the virus was beginning to build across the world. Even then I did not anticipate how things were about to unfold. I was so blind to what was about to happen that Rhian and I took a long-planned trip to Sri

Lanka on 14 March 2020. I was well aware that fear of the virus was rising because of its spread worldwide, but never in my wildest imagination did I anticipate that there would be a worldwide lockdown with all drawbridges raised.

At the beginning of March 2020, occupancy rates at Sumalee were significantly lower compared to the norm for that time of year. In Thailand, the month of March is still considered high season for visitors. It only dawned on me as to how serious things were when we arrived in Sri Lanka to be greeted by personnel in hazmat suits. At that time, somehow, Asia generally was focused on Europeans, believing they were primarily responsible for the virus spread. We hold British passports and were allowed to enter Sri Lanka after temperature checks and completing health declaration forms. Within six hours of our arrival, Sri Lanka closed its borders to British citizens.

Things happened rapidly from there. Students who were due to arrive at Sumalee contacted me to let me know that they had been advised by their governments not to travel. Students who were already staying at Sumalee started an exodus on the advice of their governments. Within a few days, Sumalee had emptied.

Rhian and I had our own problems to deal with. We were due to fly out of Sri Lanka on 28 March. I realised that the situation was escalating so on 17 March I tried to get hold of Singapore Airlines to change our flight. It was impossible to do so. I therefore made another booking for 21 March with a view to claiming a refund for the original flight.

Later the same day, a monk at a local temple we visited advised us that the Sri Lankan international airport was closing to all flights the next day. I thought he had lost touch with reality! An hour or so later, a friend sent me a link to a newspaper report confirming that the monk was correct.

We rushed back to the hotel to change our flights once again. By that time, it was impossible to get hold of Singapore Airlines or any other airline. The usual route from Sri Lanka to Phuket is either via Singapore or Kuala Lumpur. We checked online and there was nothing available on Singapore Airlines. The Malaysian government had responded quickly to the international crisis and had already closed their borders so that was not an option.

I was becoming increasingly concerned that Thailand would close its borders before we arrived back. As we are not Thai passport holders, if that had happened it would have been difficult for us to enter the country even though we have a place of residence and a business in Phuket. To say that panic set in would be an understatement. At that stage I was prepared to do whatever it took to get back to Thailand quickly.

The only option available to us was the last flight out of Sri Lanka (18 March) on Emirates routing via Dubai. We took the last two unsold seats on the flight. This is a very indirect route. Indeed, on entering Thailand, immigration were intrigued as to why we had come this way.

Leaving Sri Lanka was an eerie experience. The airport was crammed full of people, many of whom had not been able to pre-book a flight. I often wonder what happened to them as all the planes were leaving at full capacity. Our flight left just before midnight by which time Bandaranaike International Airport was mostly hordes of returning Sri Lankan nationals no doubt feeling a great deal of relief to have arrived home just before the midnight deadline.

We arrived to find chaotic scenes at Bangkok's Suvarnabhumi Airport on 19 March. The airport was closed to all international traffic on 21 March. After an uncomfortable transit through immigration where our routing was questioned, we'd managed to re-enter just in time. Getting through the airport was challenging. All arrivals were required to download the Airports of Thailand (AOT) app and needed to register their personal and onward travel details. With the majority of returnees not in possession of a local SIM card, the pressure on the airport's free internet service was great. Staff overseeing the process were overwhelmed and rather gruff. Many arrivals were struggling, particularly elderly passengers, especially as written instructions were unclear. We were fortunate in that we had a local SIM card so we got through relatively quickly. All that remained was to get a flight to Phuket, which, compared to getting a flight out of Sri Lanka, was like a walk in the park.

In terms of time, our journey from Sri Lanka to Phuket was equivalent to a journey from London to Phuket. We were exhausted when we arrived. Our staff, who met us at Phuket airport, informed us that the local authority had requested our co-operation by closing the gym for an unspecified period. It felt as if our world was about to end. As it has transpired, the world as we knew it had indeed ended. During the first wave of the spread of Covid-19 in Thailand, all MT gyms were required to close from 24 March to 1 July 2020.

Compared with many other countries, the first wave of Covid-19 infections in Thailand was low. It was tackled with a harsh lockdown to begin with. Customer-facing businesses were required to close initially for two weeks and no movement between Tambons (sub-districts) was allowed. As we lived in a different sub-district to the gym's, it meant we were unable to visit and check our business at all. During this period, all restaurants were closed and the sale of alcohol was prohibited at all outlets in Phuket. Residents were required to stay at home unless they needed to purchase food or other essentials. In some sub-districts where the virus was more widespread, residents were required to stay at home at all times with provisions being delivered to them by the local authority. Random house-to-house temperature checks were conducted throughout the province.

After the two-week, harsh lockdown, there was a gradual re-opening of businesses. MT gyms and boxing stadiums, however, were required to close for a much longer period than most other business types. One reason for this was that a MT show held at Lumpinee stadium on 6 March 2020 was identified as a super spreader event. Despite being requested not to hold the event, the upper echelons of the Thai Army (who own the stadium) went ahead regardless. The attention of the authorities was brought to the potential of this close-contact sport, and the crowds it attracts, to spread the virus quickly.

This first three months of closure was a difficult time for all MT gyms and promotions. The majority were left without any source of income. Promotions were banned for even longer than the initial gym closures of nearly three months. Any promotions that have survived since that time have been able to do so largely as a result of sponsorship. Audiences have been severely restricted since the pandemic started. Many promotions have been held behind closed doors, relayed via television or online.

At the start of the pandemic, significant numbers of Muay Thai fighters and trainers were left high and dry. Fighters who were not officially registered with the Sports Authority received nothing. Those who were registered received only a one-off THB5,000 payment.

Those MT training staff working at gyms who had not registered them with the social security system (and a large majority were not) also received little or no support. Our staff who were registered received only three payments of THB7,500 a month during the initial forced three-month closure of MT gyms. This was much less than their typical monthly salaries made up of a fixed sum and commission earned from teaching private lessons. The amount they received from the Social Security Fund was equivalent to approximately £170 a month at the time (March to June 2020).

There has been a subsequent six-week forced closure of all MT gyms in April 2021 during a third wave of the pandemic in Thailand. On this occasion, our staff received THB5,300 from the Social Security Fund, which is approximately £120. At this time of writing at the beginning of August 2021, during the most worrying period of transmission rates in Thailand so far, gyms in Phuket are in the middle of a compulsory six-week closure. This may well be extended further. Gyms in Bangkok have been required to close for even longer than this.

During the last eighteen months of the pandemic, MT gyms have experienced at least six months of compulsory closure. In Bangkok, where the third wave of the pandemic has been more serious, the closure was for longer. There has been negligible support from central government to registered businesses, regardless of sector. Staff registered with the Social Security Fund have received the equivalent of £700 to date. The situation has been even worse for MT promotions. Many stadiums have been closed since the pandemic started, including all the major stadiums in Phuket. Promotions such as Max Muay Thai, a well-known and established event previously held weekly in Pattaya, have announced their permanent closure.

Added to the lack of support from central government, all tourism-related businesses in every sector have had to contend with the effective closure of international borders since 21 March 2020. (Phuket opened to receive vaccinated tourists without quarantine in July 2021. Already at the beginning of August 2021, this scheme is under review because of rising infections countryside. Tourists entering Phuket under this Sandbox scheme are restricted with regards to movement outside of the island.) For the first six months after border closure, only returning Thai citizens and business people were allowed to enter Thailand, under strict conditions. In October 2020, the Special Tourist Visa (STV) was introduced allowing tourists who were prepared to undertake fourteen days quarantine in an Approved State Quarantine (ASQ) facility to enter the country. To meet all the entry testing conditions as well as spend fourteen nights in quarantine adds a significant amount to the cost of a visit to Thailand. Between March 2020 and July 2021, Sumalee received only four overseas guests, all of them since October 2020.

Since the pandemic started, our staff number has significantly reduced through natural attrition. Some of our MT trainers decided they would like to return to their families in Esaan to provide whatever support they could there. Whilst we were saddened to see them go, their departure meant that we have been able to give those who remained more support and consistency. The Thai staff who have remained have been employed throughout the period. The drastic reduction in the number of students able to train with us has, however, meant that they have been working reduced hours for a reduced salary. This has been enormously hard for them as described in this video by Nin Wissett, one of our trainers. However, I can only commend the staff who have remained with us for their stoicism during this period. They have responded to the crisis with good will and good grace, trying to help wherever they can despite suffering considerable hardship themselves.

Whilst this has been an immensely difficult time for Sumalee and all tourism-related businesses in Thailand, it has been a heartening time too. We have been overwhelmed by the amount of support we have received from overseas and from local residents too. When the pandemic started and our past guests realised what we faced, donations came pouring in to help our staff and members of the local Burmese community who were left in an even worse position. In the early stages of the pandemic, thousands of Burmese workers were left with no support at all. The international community generally, both locally and overseas, has been extremely generous in the amount of assistance they have given to people living in Thailand.

Sumalee has also been blessed with monthly contributions paid by international supporters in return for access to our Patreon online platform. Their monthly subscription has given them access to a library of information, including the monthly release of the chapters from this book. The contributions have kept two Thai staff employed for the duration of the effective border closure.

In many respects, the pandemic has exposed how lacking in robustness the MT community is. Well-established gyms have closed their doors, some gym owners have returned to their home countries to find a means for income there, a few gym owners have been left bankrupt and some have had to sell their homes to survive. Not only have they lacked a safety net but also they have lacked the wherewithal to generate alternative sources of income. This was a result of circumstances as much as anything else. They were hopelessly exposed for many of the reasons outlined in this book.

At Sumalee we had recognised many years ago that the business would never be viable if we continued to focus primarily on sending fighters to promotions. Like all the MT gyms, we have been hit very hard but we did have other income streams from the yoga and food side of the business. Once the international borders closed and promotions were halted, the earnings from MT were meagre. Earnings from other aspects of the business helped to supplement us.

One thing that must have been clear to all MT businesses, particularly in tourist areas, is that we had not been paying enough attention to the local/domestic market. This is something we have given a heavy focus on since the pandemic started. We have been paying much more attention to what their needs are and ways in which we can meet them. We have made many changes ranging from rescheduling the timing of classes to changing the gym environment to make it more welcoming. Although our income is considerably reduced compared to eighteen months ago, we have been able to survive up until this time. All of the income has gone towards upkeep of the premises and keeping the remaining staff in employment, as they have been the backbone of the business for a long time. This seems like the most appropriate thing to do.

Going forward, the pandemic will continue to leave the MT business community, focused primarily on training fighters, very exposed. Assuming there is some sort of return to normality by early 2022, this will mean that by that time two years will have been taken away from the careers of already established and up-and-coming fighters. Those businesses heavily dependent on this particular income stream will need to give careful consideration as to how they can secure their futures.

Epilogue

On 1 July 2021, the government opened Phuket to overseas visitors under the Sandbox programme. Unfortunately, the timing coincided with a fourth and more damaging wave of the Covid-19 virus. The Delta strain had entered the country. The government was caught unprepared due to complacency arising from their success at controlling the virus's spread earlier on in the pandemic. Consequently, at the time Delta hit, overall vaccination rates in the country were extremely low.

In Phuket, however, an extensive vaccination programme had been put in place in preparation for the Sandox opening on 1 July. This initiative provided considerable hope to all tourism-related businesses in Phuket, including ours.

It soon became apparent, however, that all of the Muay Thai gyms offering accommodation as well as training would not be able to host students from overseas. Income from overseas students forms a large part of their revenue.

In order to participate in the Phuket Sandbox scheme, it is necessary for accommodation providers to possess a hotel licence. To my knowledge, none of the MT gym businesses in Phuket had been awarded a hotel licence. There are stringent prerequisites to qualify for a hotel licence including: business registration, appropriate planning permission, meeting environmental impact, cleanliness and safety criteria, VAT registration, registration of all staff under the social security system and work permits for foreigners involved in the business.

The Hotel Act 2004 states that it is illegal to offer short-term accommodation (i.e., less than a month) without a hotel licence. As the Sandbox programme requires visitors to stay for only 14 nights with an approved accommodation provider, the authorities would have been contravening their own laws if they'd allowed those without a licence to host Sandbox visitors. Through the Certificate of Entry to Phuket, which must be granted to visitors by the government before they enter the country, the local government had found a way to rein in accommodation businesses without a hotel licence.

The government in Phuket have long been seeking a means to clamp down on accommodation providers running their businesses illegally. They had done a sweep on such businesses in 2016. At that time, I contacted our lawyers and asked them whether we needed to comply. I was assured that as a Muay Thai gym, this was not necessary. As we had a licence to lease out rooms, I was told we were covered. In fact, this was not the case. In consequence, five years later, valuable Sandbox months were lost during the period when we had to apply for the hotel licence.

The good news is that we were awarded the hotel licence very quickly as our business met all of the criteria. As we already had the prerequisites in place, we only needed to gather all the documentation and submit them to the three levels of local government in Phuket: Tambon, Amphur and City.

Such an initiative by the local government may well herald things to come. A requirement for all shiort-term accommodation providers to have a hotel licence would impact heavily on the majority of MT gyms, especially those in tourist hubs. It would necessitate either a complete change of business practice within MT gyms or the loss of a very valuable income stream from overseas students.

With an unprecedented worldwide pandemic such as Covid-19, it's difficult to predict how the future will look. In different ways, Covid-19 has changed forever the business operating environment. Tightening up on business regulations may well be an unexpected outcome in Thailand.

The digital version of the book contains hyperlinks to the online resources referred to in the text. These have been consolidated into a resource page on our website: https://sumaleeboxinggym.com/fighting-for-success-resources/

A gallery of photographs can be found on this page of our website: https://sumaleeboxinggym.com/fighting-for-success-gallery/

Acknowledgements

This book would not have been possible without the help and encouragement of family, friends and acquaintances. The following people deserve special mention: my daughter-in-law, Harriet Kilduff, for proofreading and editing the first draft of the manuscript; my daughter, Rhian, for advising on cultural issues; Dianne Buerger, who so generously gave her time and knowledge in editing the book; Lesley Naylor, who provided guidance in the final stages of the project; Dale Evans for her insight and suggestions throughout; Alan Beal for suggesting the title for the book; Steve Rosse for his rewrite of the back cover copy. I also owe a debt of gratitude to the volunteers who read the early drafts of the book and who provided valuable feedback: Matt Lucas, Marcus Haig, Patrick Valour, Lesley Naylor and Sam Miller. Finally, I am grateful for Cover Art Design by Semnitz for the cover design and to Eldes Tran for the final proofread, suggestions and edits.

Index

8LimbsUs, 68, 70

Adelphi Hotel, 15
age, respect for, 32, 69–70, 152–55. *See also* Thai culture
AKA Thailand, 45, 160
America, 85, 91, 117–18
Americans in Thailand, 1, 29, 35
Audley, Simon, 15
Australia, 75, 85

Bali, 163
Bangkok Post, 66, 119
Bangkok, Muay Thai scene in, 45, 70, 79, 81–82, 88, 97, 107–10, 112–13, 118, 120, 122, 145, 166, 189; tourism in, 1, 3–5, 79, 130
Bangla Boxing Stadium, 7–8, 10–12, 84, 97, 120–21, 125, 127, 134
Benfleet Muay Thai, 14–15
Bishop, Cindy, 67
Boughanen, Youssef, 82
boxing, 160
brand building, 11, 90, 93–95, 98–99, 103, 144, 166–72
Britain, Muay Thai scene in, 10, 14–17, 82, 85, 91–92, 102–3

Buakaw, 106–7, 109, 111
Buddhism, 55, 74, 177–78
Burmese, 75, 191
business in Thailand, buying of, 29–30; investing in, 21–26, 28–29, 31–32, 34, 37–38, 40, 48–49, 56–57, 76, 115; setting up of, 21–23, 25–26, 35–38, 51, 74–75, 173

Calzaghe, Joe, 173
Chiang Mai, 90
Chiang Rai, 8, 12
China, 74–75, 85, 91, 113, 115, 184
Chipchase, Jonno, 16
Coelst, Sunny, 167
commission, 22
communication barriers, 20, 22, 33–34, 37–40, 47, 64, 72–75. *See also* Thai culture, Thai language
conflict resolution, 47, 65, 72, 100, 111, 154–55
Copper Milk Creative, 171–72
Covid-19 pandemic, impact of, ix–xii, 6–7, 20, 22–24, 26, 45–46, 62, 114, 136–37, 162, 165–66, 176, 181, 184–95
customer service, 46, 73, 100

Davis, Mike, 94, 166–67, 170
Deachkalon Sor Sumalee (Oron), 5, 7–11, 18, 140–43, 161; in UK, 9–17
defamation laws in Thailand, 27–28, 107, 145
Digital Marketing Institute, 171
digital marketing, 71, 78, 90, 93–94, 99, 118, 144, 166–72
drug abuse, 72, 101, 146–48, 180, 182

Esaan, 9, 12, 88, 138, 140–44, 182
ethics, 10, 17, 33, 36, 38, 107, 115
Europe, 75, 85, 117
Evolve Gym, 141

Facebook, 11, 17, 118, 167–69, 182
fight purses, 12, 60, 71, 88–89, 91–93, 96–99, 109, 128, 136, 161
fighter contracts, 89, 95–96, 101, 106–16
fighters, naming of, 7–8
foreign Muay Thai fighters, 88–95, 102, 104–5, 119, 122, 126–27, 135–36, 143–46, 168, 194–95
foreign-owned Muay Thai gyms, 24, 70–72, 74, 76, 95, 99, 160, 169–70
foreigners living in Thailand, 20–23, 28, 37, 63, 66, 78, 90, 94, 136, 146, 148, 156, 158–59, 173–75, 178

gambling, 31, 41, 60, 71, 98, 108, 124–25, 136, 180
Gashi, Valdet, 126

gender inequality in Thailand, 32, 62–63, 66, 68–70, 118–21, 139–40. *See also* women in Muay Thai
Goldberg, Bradley, 10
Gosling, Colin 14

Harrison, Liam, 16, 82, 85
Hays Recruitment Consultants, 59
Hickman, Paul, 167
Hong Kong, xi, 6, 91, 167, 182
Howell, Will, 171–72
human trafficking, 106

Instagram, 169
Interval International, 5
investing in Thai business. *See* business in Thailand, investing
Iquezangkor, 128
Islam, 130, 134, 177
Izuzu Cup, 91

Japan, 85
Jays, Evan Foster, 15
Jompoplek, 9, 140–41
Jujitsu, 160
JW Marriott Resort & Spa, 4–6

Kaenchai Fairtex, 161
King's Cup, 91, 117
Klaew Thanikul, 112
Koh Phang Ngan, 90
Koh Samui, 79, 90, 97, 102, 120, 166
Kong Samui, 128
Kuala Lumpur, 3, 133, 186
Kunlun Fight, 117

labour laws in Thailand, 28, 38, 44, 61–63, 73, 75–76, 114–15
Laguna Beach Resort, 3, 5
Lamnamoon, 9, 140–43
Land Office, 30, 36
lease contract, 27, 30, 36
Legend of Victor, 117
Lerdsila, 161
Lim Chi Bin, 126
Limited Company (Ltd Co.), setting up of, 28–29, 35–36
Liverpool, 15
LNg, Mike, 83
Lucas, Matt, 169
Lumpinee Boxing Stadium, 45, 77, 79, 88–89, 97–98, 118, 120, 165–66, 188
Lumpini (promotion), 91
Lumpini Gym, 10, 14

Malaysia, 3, 91–92, 98, 124, 133, 162, 176, 186
Marriott Vacation Club, 2–6
Max Muay Thai, 89, 91, 117, 166, 189
McAdam, Douglas, 16
McLachlan, Keith, 16
migrant workers, 75–76, 181, 191
Miller, Lynne, facing misogyny, 70, 118–21, 126, 129, 133; in first Muay Thai gym partnership, 18–19, 31–33, 39–51, 62–65, 68–69, 72, 80–81, 83–84, 113, 121, 123, 170; life in Thailand, 8, 11–12, 18–19, 153–54, 173–83; life in UK, 2, 3, 8, 12–13. *See also* Sumalee Boxing Gym, Sumalee Phuket

Miller, Rhian, ix, xi, 2–3, 6, 10–11, 18–19, 51, 163–64, 172, 183–85; and Thai language, 5, 8–9, 64, 74, 83, 112, 174, 177
Miller, Sam, xi, 2–3, 6, 16, 163, 174
mixed martial arts (MMA), 45, 118, 160
Miyakoshi, Soichiro, 82
Muay Siam, 111
Muay Thai, as national sport, ix, 45–46, 78, 82, 165, 168; growth of, 7, 26, 70–71, 78–79, 82, 90, 128–29, 135, 141, 160, 165, 168–69; scoring of, 122, 179–80
Muay Thai gyms, business of, x, 20, 26, 31–34, 37–38, 42, 45–46, 53, 56, 60–62, 70, 73–74, 76, 80, 87, 89, 95, 104, 113–14, 121, 135–37, 161–62, 191, 193–95; hierarchy of, 41–42, 69–70, 72–73, 99–100, 138, 153–56
Muay Thai gyms, types of: commercial, 71, 87, 90, 95, 135–36; traditional, x, 20, 26, 31–33, 38, 42, 57, 60–62, 69–72, 87, 90, 99
Muay Thai tourism, 7, 11, 24, 64, 70–71, 78–79, 83, 87, 89–90, 95, 97, 113–14, 135, 160, 165, 168–69, 193–95
MX Muay Extreme, 91, 117

Nai Harn Gym, 11
Nai Harn. *See* Phuket
Nakhon Ratchasima, 82
Nakhon Si Thammarat, 108, 125
Narathiwat, 129–32, 161
National Stadium, 82

Nokweed Davy, 138
Num Noi, 124
nutrition. *See* Sumalee Phuket nutritional programme

O'Brien, John, 17
Omnoi Stadium, 98, 118
One Championship, 118
Oron. *See* Deachkalon Sor Sumalee
Orono Por Muang Ubon, 143

Padsaenlek Sor Sumalee, 143
Panomrunglek, 9
Parinya, 161
Patong Boxing Stadium, 127, 134–35
patriarchy, 67, 69, 99, 118–21, 139–40, 149. *See also* gender inequality in Thailand, women in Muay Thai
Pattaya, 1, 2, 79, 189
Patthalung, 123–24
Payak Samui, 128
Payakdam, 161
Penang, 3, 133–34
Petchboonchu, 178
Petchrungrueng, 128
Phromthep Muay Thai, 45, 160
Phuket Beach Club, 4, 5
Phuket Top Team, 45, 160
Phuket, living in, 1, 8, 10–11, 18–19, 24, 36–37, 76, 156–59, 174–75; Muay Thai scene in, 7, 11, 15, 18, 25–26, 31, 45, 50, 79, 90, 92, 97, 104, 108, 110, 112, 120–21, 124–25, 134–36, 160, 166, 168–69, 181, 189, 193–95; tourism in, 4–7, 24, 31, 79, 90, 162, 166, 170, 175, 181, 189–90, 193–95
Pinca, Fabio, 82, 85
Pinto, Victor, 128
PK Saenchai Gym, 85
Por Pramuk Gym, 107
Porsarnae, 165
Prayuth Chan-ocha, 67
promoters, x, 50, 96, 98, 104, 108–9, 120–23, 126–27, 141, 143–44; influence of, 89, 96, 122
promotions, 91, 98, 116–137, 161, 178, 188–89, 191; cost of, 84, 134–35. *See also* Thai Fight, Z1
Provit Aor Piroyapinyo, 128

Queen's Birthday, 117
Queen's Cup, 91

Rajadamnern Stadium, 79, 88–89, 166
Rawai Muay Thai, 160, 168
recruitment in Thailand, 59, 61–63, 72–73
Red Shirts, 13
Ridgwell, Joshua, 15
Rung Karnphan, 16
Russia, 75

Saenchai, 43, 77–86, 113, 128, 133, 135, 178–79
Saiyok Pumpanmuang, 84, 135, 178
Samart Payakaroon, 122, 125
Sandbox programme, 190, 193–94. *See also* Covid-19 pandemic
Sandee Thailand, 93, 167

200

Sanitsuda Ekachai, 119
Sek Loso, 128
sexual harassment, 65–68, 139–40. *See also* women in Muay Thai
Singapore, 3, 141, 186
Singpatong Sitnumnoi Gym, 124
social media, 11, 16–17, 27–28, 46, 71, 79, 90, 93–95, 97, 100–1, 118, 141, 144–46, 150, 165–72, 182; bad behaviour on, 54–56, 100, 103, 144–46. *See also* digital marketing
Songchai Rattanasuban, 141
Sor Sumalee Gym (SSG), 9, 18, 140–41
South Korea, 125–27
South Thailand insurgency, 129–32
Southampton, 10, 14
sponsorship of fighters, 50, 80, 85, 87–105, 122, 135–36, 145, 151–52, 163, 180–81
Sports Authority, 89, 108–9, 112–13, 136, 188
Sri Lanka, 184–86
Stadium Negara, 133
Sudsakorn, 178
Sumalee Boxing Gym (Sumalee Phuket), early days of, 51–56, 64, 90, 160, 162, 170, 174; opening of, ix–x, 1, 6, 18–20, 26, 30, 35–37, 50–51, 70, 150–51, 173
Sumalee Phuket, evolution of, x–xi, 19, 26, 37, 160–72, 174, 191; nutritional programme, x–xi, 37, 45, 162–63, 191; sponsorship of fighters, 90–105, 117–18, 129, 142–43, 145, 161, 181; staff of, xi–xii, 53–56, 59–60, 71–76, 161, 181, 188–89, 190–91; trainers of, 52–56, 60, 70–73, 100, 108–10, 121, 141, 155, 161, 167, 182, 190; yoga programme, x, 37, 45, 163–65, 191
Super Muay Thai, 117
Superlek Sorn Esaan, 9; funeral of, 127, 140–44

Thai culture, xi, 7–8, 20, 22, 32–33, 41, 47, 65, 68, 72, 99, 144, 152–55, 176–78; and business, 22–23, 29, 31–33, 39–41, 46, 57, 150–51
Thai Fight, 82, 85, 89, 91, 98, 102, 104, 107, 117–18, 127–33, 176–78
Thai language, 5, 20, 22, 64, 74–75, 176–77
Thomas, Emma, 66, 119
Thompson, Reece, 15
Tiger Muay Thai, 45, 160, 169
time-shares, 2, 4–5
Toomey, Sean, 10, 14–15, 17
Top King World Series, 91, 117, 127
tourism business, 24–25, 162, 169–70, 184–85, 187, 189–90, 193–95. *See also* Muay Thai tourism
Toyota Cup, 91, 117, 127
trainers, culture around, 60–61, 64–66, 68–69, 71–74, 95, 99–100, 103–4, 124, 138–40, 154–56
Twitter, 169

Ubon Ratchathani, 9, 18, 52, 127, 140–44
Ultim8 Fightwear, 93, 167
Ultimate Fighting Championship, 116
United Front for Democracy Against Dictatorship (UDD), 13
United Kingdom. *See* Britain

Vaynerchuk, Gary, 118
Vice, 138
videography, 11, 16, 78, 94–95, 97, 167. *See also* brand building, digital marketing, YouTube
Vietnam, 1, 85, 91, 128, 176
von Duuglas-Ittu, Sylvie, 68–70, 153

wai khru, 142
WAKO PRO World Challenge, 125–27
Watthanaya, Frances and Boom, 182

weight cutting, 15, 69, 123, 163, 180
Wissett, Nin, 190
women in Muay Thai, 46, 66, 68, 91–92, 97, 118–21, 139–40. *See also* gender inequality in Thailand, patriarchy
Wor Watthana gym, 182
work permits for foreigners, 21, 28, 42, 44, 75–76, 171, 194
World Boxing Council (WBC), 10
World Muay Thai Council, 112

Yingluck Shinawatra, 107
Yodbuangam, 161
Yodkhun, 161
yoga. *See* Sumalee Phuket yoga programme
Yokkao, 17
YouTube, 16, 79, 93–94, 167–69

Z1 International, 98, 128, 133